Waking Up in America

Waking Up In America

The Possibility of an
Earthy Enlightenment
Amidst All the Excess,
the Stress, the Pleasure,
and the Pain

Ken Taub

WHITE CLOUD PRESS

Printed in Canada

First White Cloud Press edition: 2004

Cover art: Gary Overacre
Cover concept: Ken Taub
Front cover design: Joe Girgus and Elena Kariyannis

Library of Congress Cataloging-in-Publication Data
Taub, Ken.Waking up in America : the possibility of an earthy enlighten-ment amidst all the excess, the stress, the pleasure, and the pain /
by Ken Taub. p. cm.
ISBN 1-883991-61-7 (pbk.)
1. Taub, Ken. 2. Spiritual biography--United States. 3. Spiritual life--United States. I. Title.
BL73.T35A3 2004
294.3'927'092--dc22
2004003651

The trademarked products mentioned in this book, TIME magazine, HBO, Jeep, People magazine, Studio 54, Biography, the movie "A League Of Their Own," and Cheerios, are products that the author largely appre-ciates. While not constituting an endorsement, their mention does repre-sent a vote of confidence, and one generally satisfied consumer.

This book is dedicated to those who have nurtured me the
most, my grandmother Jennie, my mother Mollie,
and my wife Lesa. . .

And to those who taught me by word or example:
Alan Watts, Allen Ginsberg, Gary Snyder,
Shunryu Suzuki, Philip Kapleau, Charlotte Joko Beck,
John Daido Loori, Bonnie Myotai Treace, Geoffrey Shugen
Arnold, and Peter Muryo Matthiessen.

The author also wishes to thank author Judy Ayyildiz, Bonnie
Myotai Treace, Sensei, and the editors of White Cloud Press
for their comments, suggestions, and much appreciated
support. In more ways than one, their interest and substantive
input have made this book not only better, but possible.
One hudred bows to each and every one.

Contents

"We were born before the wind,
also younger than the sun;
and the bonny boat was one,
as we sailed into the mystic..."
VAN MORRISON

"When you are convinced that all the exits are blocked,
either you take to believing in miracles or you stand still
like the hummingbird. The miracle is that the honey is
always there, right under your nose, only you were too
busy searching elsewhere to realize it. The worst is not
death but being blind, blind to the fact that everything
about life is in the nature of the miraculous."
HENRY MILLER

"We have not ceased from our exploration,
And the end of all our exploring
Will be to arrive where we started
And know the place for the first time."
T. S. ELIOTT

Foreword

There are now many books about Buddhism and mindful living written by Zen priests, Tibetan Lamas and Asian monks. There are scores of books about Buddhist meditation, the Buddha, and what the Buddha might do if he was alive and dating in a big city today. There are books about spectacular enlightened beings from faraway places and times past who are suddenly accessible to that author; magic beings here to soothe the perpetually unsettled modern mind. Then there are a great host of books about attaining quick and painless inner harmony, not unlike instant mashed potatoes, with the butter flavor already inside the package.

This is not one of them.

This book is about what the Buddha's insights, Ken's own insights, years of study and meditation, and intermittent Zen practices, have meant for the life of one very rambunctious fellow. What can hard-won insights from another who lived long ago and in a very different culture really mean for someone who is unquestionably modern, skeptical, judgmental, pleasure-seeking, pleasure-finding, capitalistic, suburban, sometimes edgy, sometimes poetic, completely omnivorous, and at times wildly rebellious?

I have attempted to write a book not only about my own experiences, but about the place many of us actually live as the place we must start from. Few of us have spent a year in Nepal, India or Burma with some Great Master, or three years tucked inside in a monastery, or six years, alone, in the wilderness. Most of us have busy, hectic lives filled with conflict, present obligations, and past deeds we might prefer, thank you very much, not to talk about. Most of us occupy a shaky ground which is alternately confusing, frightening, conflict-ridden, and so fraught with anxiety or uncertainty. Life moves fast, life is demanding, life is difficult. There is no one prayer, chant, or regimen that has ended our personal travails, our very human suffering, once and for all. We are now in the 21st century, we are moderns, we are savvy, and we have seen it all, or nearly so. We know better.

Or do we? Almost everyone I know has more than anxiety and uncertainty stirring inside. Most of us have an intriguing and persistent voice deep within, similar to a hidden wellspring of wisdom, that whispers to us as we rush through our lives (or sometimes bubbles up with urgency), that there is more, that *we* are more, that there is great majesty and a wondrous mystery here — *right here* — and that life does not have to be so damned hard.

This book is about how one person responded to that voice.

PART I

Mistaken Identity
(or Crouching Monkey, Hidden Buddha)

I

"KNOCK-KNOCK...."

EARLY MORNING IN EARLY MARCH. I'm looking into the bathroom mirror at my unshaven face. Often times I'm inclined to ignore my face, but once in a while I study it, as if through a large magnifying glass. This morning I scan a few pores, the profile of my nose, and then bare my teeth. I study the landscape of my face, the skin stretched over my skull, with that odd mix of concern and detachment. I have been observing this ever-changing face for what feels like forever. Still, I look at this face as if it were a mask or a separate entity. My thoughts quickly wander from "Boy, I need a shave" to a kind of vague yet persistent wonderment: "Who is that?" "What's behind that face beside blood and bone and brain?" "Really now, who's there?" I return to familiar ground and settle on the more immediate notion that I need a shave before work. I walk toward the kitchen to make coffee, where I am greeted by my then 3-year old son. He has just arisen, and with a smile on his face and out of nowhere—one of the many brilliant specialties of small children—he calls me Dusthead.

I like the name. It fits. I am tickled by a mix of astonishment and appropriateness. That night, in my journal, I write only these three words: Call me Dusthead.

At first, I want to put this new name on my license plates, or carve it into a wood plaque and hang it over the door to my office. I think the better of such plans, and just sit with the name. Finally, after a few days, I smile that broad, satisfied smile when it hits me, but nicely, that Dusthead is more than a cute nickname given to me by my son. Newly groomed or unshaven, Dusthead is who I am. Dusthead, ancient and empty, is the who-less who that sits behind my skull and beneath my heart. I continue to reside within this vague something—part feeling, part observation—and see what emerges. A few days later, this is what comes out:

Call me Dusthead. For as long as I can remember I have gone where the wind goes. I have followed the currents. First the clouds, then the rivers, then the animal tracks, and finally the fields of flowing grain. I have rolled up the hillsides and I have rolled into the hollows. When I enter a town or a city most of the occupants ignore me, or they look at me as if I was a foolish creature. Perhaps they are right, but it does not much matter. I am never alone. Now the wind goes where I go. I watch the landscape and the animals, and there are days when the birds and the beasts follow me, and times when the clouds race alongside me, and laugh.

I have moved about for thousands of years, surely for longer than any one being can retain in any one head. I keep moving, moving. First here, then there. In this manner and in that. Even if I am foolish, I am intimate with each eddy, rush and swirl, and it seems that every current knows my name. The tides move in and whisper, I step forward and whisper. I wink and nod, the tides wink and nod. We seem to understand one another. Either way, it is a very ancient dance, older than the mist.

I continue to move. I have gone north and south, up mountains and into lush valleys yet again for nearly the last half century. Now there have been times when I have forgotten who I am, lost in various activities or new titles, but sooner or later I shake myself free and remember. Other times, something just hits me in the head.

I may be raking the soil or discussing current events. I may live quietly in the woods or race past the ocean. But it does not matter much. I realize I keep busy because we are inclined to be busy, or in order to pay for a meal, or to engage other beings, or to occupy time. I am surely not this occupation or that preoccupation. I am Dusthead. I am only Dusthead. I will be Dusthead this moment, and the next moment, and into the long tomorrow.

Every morning we awaken and quickly become ourselves. Even before we wash our face or finish our first cup of coffee, our memories, defenses, and day-to-day personality converge and begin to function along with our eyes, muscles, and appetites. That which we take ourselves to be, the carefully constructed self that we all call "me," puts on a persona like we put on a shirt. It happens automatically, requiring no more advance planning than taking our next breath. I get up and Ken Taub gets up with me. All of us have painstakingly formed an identity that we believe suits us—indeed, we believe *is* us—and we mostly walk through the world and our lives in this haze of mistaken identity. Every day, we awaken in almost every way but to our deeper awakened being.

Yet there is a voice inside of all of us—sometimes a whisper and at other times a shout—that points to something far deeper than individual personality, or even our own personal histories. The problem is that we generally view this undefined *Something* as if we are looking at a distant light through a dense fog. The essential core of our being can seem farther away from us than Tibet.

All of us have felt this profound estrangement and pervasive disconnect. Modern people call it alienation, but this irksome feeling is something more intrinsic than contemporary alienation from nature or other people. When it comes to our own selves, we are as people who still see the world as "flat" because that is what it appears to be. Just as the ancients misperceived the shape of our world and the order of our solar system, so do we moderns misperceive ourselves and our place in the world. On occasion, we may be enticed by the stories of great sages, potent hints from wiser sources, or even our own intuitive flashes of something deeper than the world of appearances. Indeed, most of us sense that we are intrinsically connected to the rest of the world and the larger cosmic oscillations; that there is a way of being that is somehow "more full or more real." Yet a great and borderless Mystical Union runs counter to our daily experience—and excuse us, we have jobs, families, bills, and we're quite busy. Our everyday minds have trouble with what the mystics, transcendentalists, yogis, and saints have proclaimed for many centuries. And it is quite understandable.

Yet for those who care to look deeper and to listen, there are also reports that a few of us, including some of our own fellow citizens, have discovered and now occupy the real "round" world. Their lives are no longer flat or shallow or shrouded in a hazy mist. They are not alienated. They live not apart. They are awake.

This is how the story goes:
Mahakashyapa, a disciple of Siddhartha Gautauma, the Buddha, watched as the great sage from northern India twirled a single flower between his graceful fingers, and winked. Mahakashyapa caught the eye of the Buddha and smiled. In that very instant, the Buddha knew there was someone who could move forward with the pure flower of enlightenment and guide others back to their own intrinsic nature. Mahakashyapa had practiced along with the other monks and respectfully followed what he was instructed to do. He meditated, bowed formally, performed his chores, and payed homage to the Buddha, as did the other followers. But he went much farther than that. "Thousands of times Mahakashyapa had pounded his bones and crushed his body. His face was no longer his own. Thus he received the Buddha's face by means of face-to-face transmission."[1] Pure, unadorned awareness had met pure, unadorned awareness, and there they were, and here we are.

Great leaders, countless cities and whole cultures have come and gone in the past 2,500 years, while the Buddha's teachings on the eleviation of existential suffering and dread, on deeper awareness and the innate compassion that awareness engenders, has moved from India to China, Tibet and southeast Asia, from China to Korea and Japan, and finally to Europe and America. There is, in

---

1 Eihei Dogen, edited by Kazuaki Tanahashi, "Face-to-Face Transmission" from *Moon In A Dewdrop* (New York: North Point Press, 1998), p. 176.

short, an entire *culture of awakening* that has been passed like a torch from century to century and from place to place. The Buddha, along with a few outstanding mystics and sages of other traditions, has unequivocally layed out the groundwork and pointed to the right tools. If one has the will, there is surely The Way.

Now one does not have to go far to find The Way. I love the expression that *enlightenment is naught but the lighting of a candle in a well lit room* because I have found it to be true, and after Buddha lit the first candle, that candle lit another candle, and so on and so forth, from that time to the next time and on up to this very day. Again, the candle of enlightenment is there for us to grab if only we choose to. One can choose St. Francis', or Rumi's, or Meister Eckhart's, or Ramana Maharshi's, or Martin Buber's, or a dozen other time-tested candles. Despite what the fundamentalists have to say, these great teachings are but branches of the same tree. The underlying philosophy, the vital source, while wearing several masks, runs ancient and deep. As for me, I have had a strong inclination toward the teachings of the Buddha and to Zen Buddhism for most of my life. Not forgetting the fact that this man lived in India over 2,500 years ago, and that I have never taken Buddhist vows or otherwise converted, what he expressed speaks to my modern heart, while Zen speaks more to my head (actually, it often "hits me in the head" to break up thinking which is thickly padded with fear or conditioning).

Of course it is a new time, and for most of us life is quite different than it was over two millennia ago. Things have changed so very dramatically in just the last one hundred years. The space shuttle breaks free of our atmosphere routinely and we are connected everyday to the next city or to Asia or Europe by our home computers. So can we space travelers have the eyes and ears of Mahakashyapa? How do we busy moderns hooked to modems "pound our bones and crush our bodies"? What might have to happen for scientific materialists living in a world of extraordinary skyscrapers, cell phones, fertilization clinics and astrophysics to turn ourselves inside out, "lose our face," and find our Original Face?[2] Is it realistic to expect people who move at such speed and who live life with such hasty burdens on their shoulders to find the time to release the self, gain insight into our deepest nature, merge with this great *Something* and then reenter our information-packed, sound-tracked, forever-noisy lives? Can there really be modern mystics? If so, can a 21st century mystic still function effectively; still watch satellite TV and balance the books; still spend forty-five hours a week inside the glass and steel shrines of capitalism and then return home, usually in traffic, to raise our unrestrained digital offspring? Can an honest-to-goodness mystic still engage in honest-to-goodness erotic play? Do buddhas make whoopy?

If the answers are yes, then more questions arise. When we are willing to challenge that which we know, what we are sure of and take for granted, and are willing to sacrifice our carefully constructed personalities, what will be left to guide us? If we ask, "Knock, knock, who is it?' and some voice very deep within answers, almost trembling, "I don't know," what then? If the great Something becomes the great Nothing will there be anything

2. See Glossary in back (pp.141-147) for definition of Zen terms as they appear in the text.

remaining but a bottomless, forbidding void? As we embark on this supremely interior voyage, are we also disregarding the Creative Force that transcends space and time, the One most of us call God?

Without our prior net of beliefs, it might seem like we are apt to fall down into a dark pit, or collapse into some sort of unrecognizable mess. Or might something else happen? When we go deep enough will we discard our no longer necessary disguises and defenses, begin to understand our intrinsic nature and our place here on this grand planet, and thus awaken to greater freedom and previously unimagined possibilities? Enlightened beings in a turbulent, competitive, high-speed world? What will become of us?

I don't know what will become of you. That is the honest answer. What I can tell you is what has happened to me.

2

On The Road, Again

WE ALL HAVE OUR STORY. We all live an unfolding tale that alternately informs and confounds us. We occupy what appears to be the time line of our lives, beginning, we are told, on the day that we exit our mother's womb. But my brief story will be less about that time or this place, or my own colorful family history, and more about my odyssey, an inward looking adventure that continues to this day.

I'm not sure of when I began this odyssey. Perhaps it was at age 15 when I started thumbing through Herman Hesse's 1931 novel *Siddhartha* at a friend's house. Or was it soon afterwards, when I borrowed—for 33 years—another friend's copy of Paul Reps' wonderful compilation, *Zen Flesh, Zen Bones*? In a more obvious way, it could have been the day, a month shy of turning 17, I hitchhiked up the coast of California and headed east from the dazzling parcels of earth and shore that is Big Sur to arrive at the newly opened Tassajara Zen Mountain Center. Or maybe this odyssey began when I asked my first "how did we get here?" question. As a preteen I began to question things a great deal, wondering about God and the universe and our place in it. Or was it, in fact, the day I left a maternity ward in Brooklyn? Is that when this odyssey began, at birth?

Now I listen to those breezy voices of the old Chinese and Japanese Zen adepts, and to the sound of the wind blowing through all the space around and within me, and hear tell that this odyssey began before I was born, before I had this face. So maybe the wind knows. Then again, its possible that an essential kernel of myself was born before the wind itself was born, and so the tale I tell and the events I seam together will be of compelling interest to the wind, or failing that, amusing.

I think the wind hears me. To be sure, there are times I actually stand still long enough to hear it.

One thing I am absolutely certain about is this: the odyssey continues. As a young man, I thought one day you reached satori, ultimate enlightenment, and you broke out in a mix of exultant tears and ecstatic laughter, and that the world remained only crystal clear and that you never had a moment of sorrow or a crease in your brow from that luminous instant on.

Perhaps that is what happened to a few people, but not to me. I was not only a curious lad, I was a rebellious one. You couldn't tell me much, I had to find things out for myself, frequently chin first. While the revolutionary teachings of Siddhartha Gautauma, the Buddha, and the Zen pracitioners I met early on opened a vast new door for me, I remained a rebel, albeit a half-assed one, and lived much of my life like a lusty sailor at port and not like some peaceable Chinese sage humbly joined with my immediate surroundings.

This unruly boy was also a bit of a native philosopher, and I did a fair amount of reading and no shortage of pondering. Just the same, I was no exception, and like most seekers, greater confusion certainly preceded any real clarity. But this is no sin, or if it is, it is an easily forgivable one. After all, we take this journey not only with our feet and our legs but with the rest of our body. We take this journey with our pasts, our culture, our fears, and our potent appetites. Yet beyond human desire and personal history, the toughest part is that we take the journey with our minds.

Now while the mind is a wonderful thing to have when you want to cross the street safely or figure out a mathematical equation, the mind becomes a peculiarly messy hindrance when you wish to see the unity of all the seemingly disparate things and the inherent selflessness of the self. When you embark upon a journey to a place where, finally, there is no "there" there, its not hard to see how a person can become disoriented (just ask the theoretical physicists).

What do we do? We turn to our compasses. And what is our compass of first and last resort? Our mind and its constructs. So this is what the unruly boy was finally forced to do to move forward and advance: study my conditioning and my constructed self. Emptiness, unadorned awareness and Dusthead were barely even glimpsed for quite a few years. I always had a full tank, preferring to zoom ahead at full speed. I perpetually recreated and so had to live with the Ken Taub Show on a daily basis. To be sure, it was wildly amusing at times but it was often a thicket—or rather a net that I wove and then chose to dive into. I still live with the images and perennial reruns of that show, but today things are different. I now know who writes, produces and acts in the show. But I did not know that years back. It seemed like my issues came from "back then" or "out there."

Early on, from a very young age, I felt like another anxious little being swimming upstream. At age 4 or 5, my mother labeled me "the fish." But I was not just a good swimmer for a little guy, I was a fish hellbent on survival. I was also hungry. I was always hungry for attention, and yearning for affection. Fortunately, a few years later, another kind of yearning arose, took residence and resided just below the surface. I yearned to understand my nature on a deeper level.

But what did I do initially? I engaged in another athletic diversion: I ran.

Right after my parents separated, I tried running away at age 5. In elementary school, I won a blue ribbon for the 50 yard dash. I ran away from high school for a brief time (more on this in a bit). I ran from New York to California, and then I ran from America to Europe and the Middle East. When I arrived in Israel, I continued to run. It was there I began my jogging career. After all, why just be with one's self when one can take flight? Of course, despite the fact of inertia, an object in motion will have to slow down and stop eventually. Intermittently, I would slow down and take a good look at myself before revving up again. I did think about The Nature of Things, and about what made me tick, and run. I thought: "Okay, you big monkey, what's *really* going on here?"

The universe does not hide for the most part but it does reveal its many secrets very slowly. Nature can be one tough nut to crack. Now what about our own nature? What about this clever, chattering, mischievous, generalizing, grasping, territorial, folly-laden, superstitious, singing, dancing, endlessly aroused, alternately mean and sympathetic, and sometimes noble creature? What happens when this talking monkey begins to delve into the deeper nature *of its own nature* ? Do we gain easy wisdom or do we become unhinged? In my experience, we tend to act like a child in a dense maze. We become frightened. The grasping creature tends to grasp all the more tightly. Entering new territory and feeling bewildered, we are generally inclined to hunker down into habit, or to stuff our new experiences into the familiar comfort chest of What Is Already Known.

Eventually, we forge on. One great and positive lesson from human history is that we can in fact shift from security to the unknown. Our species has been generally excellent at moving over time from the dense brush to the open plains. We can gain insight along with our new experiences. With a new-found courage, we can study the self with enduring scrutiny and unflinching honesty, until we turn ourselves inside out. We can even go deep enough to find ourselves one day awash in a beautiful Mystery, fully realizing that we are an integral part of That which is ultimately unknowable.

But oh those touchstones of familiarity and oh those big appetites. We long for what is tangible and familiar. So it was that I returned to my richly distracting American culture, to my ample appetites for good food and sex . . . and please know I have not yet lost my lusty nature. But once I was largely a slave to it, and now I largely celebrate it. Or, I'm a slave with velvet shackles and a knowing smile.

Before I could sit still, I looked here for affirmation and there for acknowledgment, and then moved over to that spot and looked for them yet again. I still enjoy being acknowledged, it is a common trait among our kind, but the opinions of others are no true compass for my freely beating heart. And, like most people, I had longings. I longed for and enjoyed travel, adventure, play, and more play. To be sure, I relish all of them still.

But things are different for me now. Increasingly, I am aware that the first sips of cold juice in the morning and playtime in the evening are essentially pleasant phenomena, and the only intrinsic meaning they have are the ones I give to them. Of course, our brains and our tongues know what they like—we do have pleasure centers and selective taste buds—yet once I opened up more fully and *actually experienced my experiences* I was able to enjoy sucking on a lemon nearly as much as a chocolate bar (that's *nearly*). Pleasure is pleasure, we like what we like, yet ever since I have entered this door that I willingly opened, this great "gateless gate," and tasted the fruits of stillness and unadorned being it seems as if the swirling winds inside and out keep blowing me back toward that clear vista to which the Buddha's teaching pointed: the dharma, the organic truths of unfettered consciousness. For better and for worse, it is now much harder for me to solicit abandon and dive back solely into a life of distractions, fleeting pleasures, and endless *stuff*.

Please know, I love our modern life, with its conveniences, digital toys, cinema, and gourmet cuisine. And yet . . . there is something deeper underneath the glittering surfaces, and that something the core of my heart longs for as much, if not more.

So can we have it both ways? Most of us will continue

to drive our cars and go to the cinema, but can we be keenly attentive at the steering wheel or even in a movie theater? Moderns who turn their backs completely on the devices of convenience and the well hawked objects of desire are as few as diamonds in the desert. We like our toy chests. Is it possible then? Can we remain mindful as we feed our faces with popcorn staring up at the big screen? Can we drive nice cars and wear nice clothes and live in nice houses full of nice things and be clear and largely still and profoundly content in the deepest chambers of our being? *Can we balance our desire for pleasure and our desire for enlightenment*? That's *the question* for most Westerners and for Americans in particular, isn't it?

In the land built on "more, newer, better" can we dwell also in the ancient lands of emptiness, timelessness and perfection in the moment? And if so, how long does this transformation take, for goodness sake?

I was a Long Island, New York boy spending the summer in downtown Los Angeles in the small apartment of a friend of a friend, nearing the end of my sixteenth year, awash with more piss and vinegar than insight, and one day I found myself with thumb out in the July heat of 1969, the month America landed on the moon.

I was running again, this time headed up the splendid coast highways of California, filled with vague yearnings and fueled by the grand inertia that is teenage idealism, and I was looking for a place called Tassajara.

I had read about the Zen Mountain Center at Tassajara first in TIME magazine, and it had intrigued the young man who had read the American Beat poet Allen Ginsberg, the British philosopher Alan Watts, and some of the great Japanese scholar D. T. Suzuki. Zen practice remained for me a thing not unlike California: a more perfected place, a shimmering, Oz-like point to find and explore, an ideal land where tears vanished and happiness reigned supreme. Like the majority of seekers, what I really sought was a way to alleviate my personal pain. I was not so much interested in waking up or clear-seeing as I was in finding the ultimate salve for all my wounds. I didn't know this at the time. I felt a kind of nobility in my yearning, but my quest for selflessness began with selfishness; forgivable in that it is not only a common trait of teenagers but the chief motivation for almost all people who embark upon a journey of deeper discovery.

At a point just past Santa Barbara a car pulled over and a smiling face asked me where I was going. I think I simply answered "North" and the driver kindly beckoned me in. Paul Scanlon was a warm and engaging man, five or six years my senior, and at a time when a whole lot of people grinned and flashed the peace sign, giving off the facade of easy brotherhood, Paul was the real deal, genuinely friendly and considerate. But beyond that, Paul turned out to be more than my ride north, he turned out to be my entry ticket to a thriving American Zen Center. After talking about this and that, our travelers' discussion turned to philosophy and Zen and eventually to Tassajara, and sure enough Paul knew exactly where it was, and better still, he said he was going to take me there.

Clearly, I had caught the right ride. To this day, I remain largely amazed that the serious students of the Tassajara Zen Center let this unannounced, hitchhiking teenager into their community and into their zendo, if only for three days. They were generous minded and could see that I was earnest, but I remain touched all these years later that they included me in their lives and practice. As it turns out, their vast generosity altered my life.

I ate with the older students of Tassajara, I did chores with them, and I meditated with them. I can recall the dry summer central California air, the sparse mountain terrain, the revitalizing hot springs that ran right through the grounds, and I can remember the cool morning mist which parted nearly every day right about noon, mist which vanished into pale blue skies to offer a clear vista out toward the majestic Pacific coast. You did not have to be a poet or a sage to feel the land alive beneath your feet and before your eyes. All you had to do was get up early in the morning, inhale deeply, and look in any direction.

But the coastal beauty does not sit in the forefront of my memory. More than the lush, outsized landscape, I remember the young American monks. I remember their gentle mien, their quiet movements, their deliberateness, and above all their kindnesses to the truculent, wild haired, wide eyed boy that I was.

My memories of Tassajara are largely impressionistic now. They are glowing, bygone images which bob up now and again in the seas inside my skull to inform and reassure me. Over thirty years later, I feel a kind of affectionate appreciation for the teenager with a head full of grandiose, unformed ideas trying to sit still on a meditation cushion. Surely, my curiosity was much stronger than my ability to reside quietly in the moment. I mostly wanted to study faces, the details of their rituals, and how these Zen adults moved through the world. I peeked about often, including the frequent periods of meditation (guess what, sometimes I still do). As for idealistic bubbles and their bursting: the work detail I was asked to do at Tassajara was the washing of dishes, a job I recently had at a busy diner back home, and a job which I hated. It struck me that I had traveled all this way to get my first taste of Zen living, and here I was washing dishes again. So much for grandiose. Even the young man with dish towel in hand could appreciate the wise irony of the situation.

Yet my memories remain palatable ones, and although memory can be a sweet liar, I know these recollections to be honestly positive and not selectively positive.

I remember their wholesome, excellent homemade bread and the clean, light food. I remember feeling not only included but cared for. I can also recall my first encounter with the long, flat kyosaku stick that *upon one's request* with a seated bow, came snapping down on one shoulder and then the next as a form of deep muscle stimulation and as a way to be unambiguously in the present, if only for ten stinging seconds. Yet this too remains a favorable memory. I have been a hedonist for as long as I can remember, and on my better days I am just a more mindful hedonist, yet there was something about the clean austerity and the deep complexity wrapped in the black cloth of Japanese ritual and simplicity that somehow appealed to me then, and which appeal to me even more now. The single-pointedness of Zen managed to poke me in my heart and my ass at the same time. Zen and self realization are also hard work often times, especially in the beginning, but here was one spoiled American who knew instinctively that if anything was worth the time and the effort that this thing was it. Remember when Tom Hanks' character sternly lectured a distraught and tearful ballplayer in the movie "A League Of Their Own" on the undeniable fact that baseball is hard . . ."but its the hard that makes it good."

Zen is like that.

I left my three days at Tassajara a changed person. No, I was not converted.

No, I was not made newly whole. And I certainly was not instantly enlightened. But I was changed. Something uncommon had crept under my sixteen year old skin. It had no form and had no name but I surely felt it. And of course, it is with me still.

How changed was I at the time? Only three months after returning to New York from my summer of exploration in California, I took myself out of my senior year in Syosset High School and boarded a Greyhound bus for far upstate New York.

My parents were not pleased, to say the least, but I was an independent little so-and-so, and so off I ran to Rochester, which was the home of the pioneer American Zen scholar turned Zen teacher, Philip Kapleau; best known as the author of the now classic *Three Pillars of Zen*. Here was another thriving Zen center and so that is where I headed.

I arrived at the Rochester Zen Center raring to go. Raring to go where and to do what I honestly can not say, but I was sure I was ready for whatever these alert Zen types would throw at me. Having mistaken all that I was trying to avoid at home and in my life for some kind of keen determination, I just up and left high school, traveling to the northwest portion of upstate New York. Out of that special mix of adventure and avoidance my next quest was born. Soon enough, there I was with my two bags on the parlor floor of a large old home in Rochester, New York.

Happily, Mr. Kapleau, this renown teacher of Zen, was willing to see me and we chatted for a few minutes—he smiling and patient with this long haired teen with a fairly good rap—before I somehow convinced him that a conversation indoors was not the wise thing to do when the whole beautiful autumn world was waiting outside for us. It was not my infectious enthusiasm to be sure but rather Mr. Kapleau's gentle accommodation that found us both jogging down his long driveway and into the street. We were both smiling, and he was slowly running alongside me as I cheered him on, but after about fifty yards he smiled again and made a U-turn and headed back. I remember calling back to him, "Come on, come on!" but he had already honored my request, invested himself in some fresh air aerobics with this feisty young newcomer, and returned to his office. My fuzzy-headed glee turned instantly to disappointment, but I did not lose any of my ambition, no matter how vague it was, and so I followed him back to the large house. The Zen teacher had just given me his first lesson, wordless but no less worthwhile, a lesson I would not catch on to for many years to come.

To my surprise, Mr. Kapleau was kindly willing to speak to me once more. He asked me why I had come there, what I wanted to achieve, and then how old I was.

He listened attentively to my first two answers, which may have made some sense or not, but when I told him that I was 17 and had just left home and high school, he told me politely but firmly to go back home, go back to school, finish school, live my life, and *then* if I was still interested in Zen studies in ten more years to give it a go at that time. I think the blood must have drained from my face. Ten more years? I had not just dropped out and traveled over 350 miles to hear this!

Surprised, and a bit stung, I told him I had nowhere to stay, and so he gave me the name and address of one of his younger students so I could spend the night (as a measure of my great, dumb certainty that the kind practitioners would let me join their upstate Zen community, I had maybe twenty dollars in my wallet, not even enough money to get myself back home). So off I went to this fellow's rented flat, and with only mild reluctance he let me in. This was still the Sixties after all.

After dinner, I informed my young host of my present dilemma, and while we were talking I came upon a plan of action. My host agreed to it, becoming my confederate. What did he do? He grabbed a scissor and cut my hair. Off went my long, dark curls. Then he took a razor to my new crewcut, turning a 17 year old upper middle class, would-be hippie into a bald, would-be Buddhist. I looked proudly at my clean head in the mirror and smiled radiantly, as if I was the male, American, dharma-ready Joan of Arc.

The next day I returned to the Rochester Zen Center, convinced that the shining pate of my pious conviction would be so self evident that I would not be turned away from the Pearly Gates by Saint Peter, let alone from a compassionate-minded Zen center with its patient spiritual headmaster.

Of course, I was wrong. Despite my grand statement of sudden baldness, I was still not going to be welcomed into the community. In fact, after the prior's day flighty jog and this day's appearance of a chrome dome teen, Mr. Kapleau correctly assumed I was partially out of my tree, and when he tried to get one of his larger students to personally escort me out of the place I resisted, despite the student's considerable size and the clear encouragement to get lost. I was determined. Having been a high school wrestler, I was able to kick out my legs, digging my toes into the carpet in defiance. Not one to take rejection lightly, I resisted in force. As it happens, during what was surely the very first wrestling match at the Rochester Zen

Center, my wallet evidently fell out of my pocket, and so Philip Kapleau, watching ringside, quickly scooped it up and headed to the local police station to find out if I was just another teenage runaway or if I was in fact an escapee from some institution for the mentally befogged.

He returned, having found out that I was not on some wanted list, but I had to depart from the old house all the same. He saw no benefit to the center or to his students to have an alternately wild and romantic young lad infecting the premises.

I was physically unharmed, but I was crushed. I had shaved off my beloved locks in a statement of determination. I had literally fought to stay. But they said in effect, "Go southeast, young man. Go home, where you belong."

The next day there I was in an apple orchard, with a clean shaven head and a burlap sack around my torso, which was there to hold the fall apples I was picking in far upstate New York. Dejected but practical, I was picking fruit to earn my bus fare home. To this day, I can almost see myself stooped in labor at the orchids, and I am certain that I have never before or since appeared to be such a humble Zen apprentice, at least physically.

My mother, wanting to teach me a needed lesson, would not wire me the money to get home, so I topped off the money I had earned at the apple orchid with dish washing at a diner that evening (catch the pattern here?), and with the combined incomes I had enough cash for the bus ride back home. It was a long and lonely ride.

Truth be told, while I had not been able to practice at the Zen Center in order to tame my ego, the entire episode had in fact *crushed* my normally healthy ego, and I spent the long bus ride home—as well as a good deal of the next six months—somewhat disoriented and depressed. I did not really know what it was that I had gone on this youthful quest for, but I surely knew that I had failed at it.

Students at my high school were nonetheless fascinated by my brief but special adventure, while my driver's ed teacher called me Quasimoto. One wild friend of mine, despite the fashion for longer hair at the time, actually thought I looked uniquely cool with no hair, so he shaved his own head in an act of defiance and solidarity. I got used to the stares of my fellow students soon enough, and life as a senior went on. There are two pictures of me in my Syosset High School yearbook: one, smiling in white t-shirt and crewcut in the art department as my hair was beginning to grow back, and the other, my senior shot taken in the spring of 1970, of the young lad with his wicked long curls back in full regalia.

Come spring, my energetic spirits returned. My piss and vinegar and my appetite for adventure came back in force. By the time I was getting close to graduation, I had talked the parents into letting me go to college on the West Coast and I was accepted at one school in Orange County, and so come July there I was loading up my first car, a used but nearly perfect 1965 red Chevy Impala convertible. The young adventurer was packing the trunk for a return visit to California, a visit that would last seven years. I had followed Philip Kapleau's injunction to finish school and to live my life. But after starting out with a precarious mix of philosophy and psychology as my twin majors, I switched schools, moving further south to a sweet and sleepy little coastal town called Encinitas, where I would live for three years as I commuted to beautiful La Jolla to get my degree in Chinese Studies at the University of California at San Diego. My interest in metaphysics and mysticism, in Eastern philosophy and in Zen

KEN TAUB

Buddhism had not waned, but it had taken on another form.

And that, in large part, is both the beginning and the end of my story.

Surprised? Its understandable. Yet while I can fill page after page telling you about my seven years in California, my travels abroad, my life as a banana picker on a kibbutz in Israel, my return to Long Island, my interesting career in business-to-business advertising, my rich and varied love life and other unprintable topics, the people I tickled and those I rubbed the wrong way, my home town life for the past twenty years, and about my kind and lovely yoga teacher wife and beautiful young son, none of this will make much difference to you and your life when it comes to the question of waking up and to the response of mindful living. None of it.

Why? Because one's circumstances—while rarely accidental—are still just circumstances. Its fun to watch Biography on cable television or to read *People* magazine now and again. But all we glean about the person is incident and outline, plus a few interesting facts. Either we want yet more information piled on top of all the information we already have . . . or we want to wake up to our authentic self.

After all my running, and all my travels, I now know that one can wake up under most any circumstance: in one's own backyard or while hiking in the Rocky Mountains, in a poorer part of Asia or a wealthy part of London, while folding the freshly laundered towels or while hearing an acorn hit the root of its tree, while living a monastic life removed from the general fray or while going to a job and raising kids. Waking up means responding to the ancient winds whispering in your marrow and to your heart, and then seeking an end to self-perpetuated delusion.

We are motivated by our own suffering and confusion, which are powerful, until we finally make a new choice. One of the choices we can make is to finally diminish our suffering and confusion by engaging in the kind of deep inquiry and determined practice that enhances Being and exposes that Great Pretender to the throne, the charlatan of charlatans, the ego. With a combination of great effort and great stillness *we can actually change the way we listen to our own inner dialogue.*

Over time, I was able to actually hear and to see the world in a very different way by being still. Aging and life experience helped, some personal therapy did not hurt, reading some excellent books surely fed my mind, but nothing was quite as potent as getting my butt on a cushion and keeping it there for 15, 25 or 60 minutes. Remaining still, quiet and centered I found that I was moving in a natural fashion right through the prickly little demon as if he were a ghost. Quietude creates its own special kind of illumination, and when enough light is shone upon the tempestuous voice disguising itself as our self it can finally be exposed for the vacant fraud that it is. While few people become completely egoless, we can still recognize it as the fool and the charlatan it is whenever it pops up. And this recognition, this sane and correct identification, can indeed be our passport to a life of clarity, receptivity, inclusiveness, and greater empathy.

3

On the Island of Maui,
Looking for Paradise

So IF I STATE THAT THE high points and pratfalls of my own life are not particularly instructive, and there is not much more of my autobiography left to talk about here, what is it that I can tell you? Ultimately, not much. But I can tell you what my own deft maneuvers and less brilliant moves have taught me. Namely, slow down a bit. Take a good look around. Stop for just a moment. Take a deep, full breath. And pay attention.

At every moment of our lives we are in the midst of the magical, the beautiful, the raw, the challenging, and the mysterious. And the instructional. Every single moment in our lives *if given clear and sufficient attention* is an instance that can awaken us. There is the story of a rabbi who sends his disciple to another town to study with another rabbi. The disciple asks asks, "Why, to learn Torah from him?" The rabbi answers, "No, to watch how he ties his shoelaces."

If the devil is in the details then perhaps the way out of our difficulty is detailed observation of the minutiae of our lives, of the nuances and the littlest things.

Wisdom is cultivated by paying attention to the smallest detail and the smallest expressions of life.

I have a great deal of energy. I am inclined to to be an object in motion, not rest. I am full of frivolity, curiosity, and chatter. Yet I get to enjoy all of it that much more once I shut up and sit still. Quiet, one actually gets to be where one is. We get to experience, to engage, to drink in, and not just think about.

I have been to Key West and Cancun, Martinique and Maui. I have been in the middle of such lushness and splendor, and somehow managed to be somewhere else. My eyes and heart were undeniably full, yet I was still hungry. I was being nailed, lovingly, smack in the middle of my forehead with the fluttering wing of a bird of paradise, and yet I was thinking about something other than the love bird, rubbing my fool tummy, looking for God-knows-what. The Buddhists call this riding an ox looking for an ox to ride. Some also call it missing one's own life.

The Eye of the Storm, the Space Between Notes

Modern life, even on what we call a good day, is fast and hectic. Perhaps it's different elsewhere, but here in New York a lot of us feel like we are juggling five balls while peddling on a unicycle with a bent wheel. I'm not only in the New York metro area, I'm in advertising, and so if I'm only juggling five balls, I feel like it's a day at the beach. Ask someone moving at such speed to cultivate mindfulness and in these parts they'll likely tell you to "go cultivate yourself" somewhere else.

Now, I'm not completely sure why I started meditating, but I did, and to say that I'm glad that I did would be a sizeable understatement. I can also say that now I have a better idea why so many yogis, mystics, and people who could not take a long tropical vacation have engaged in meditation for the past 30 centuries, or longer.

Meditation's ripe moments of quietude and unadorned awareness are largely nurturing. They promote simple attention and a kind of quiet you can feel wash up your back. This cultivated quiet can manifest as a safe center, not unlike the eye of the storm, or the space between notes, which in their soundlessness create the music's rhythm. Meditate with consistency and an unexpected jackpot is hit time and again. The payoff of stillness and paying simple attention is large: a life that is more fully lived. One can actually do more than visit Maui, one can *be* in Maui, deeply and completely.

The expeditious marketing executive discovered firsthand the difference meditation made to his various states of mind, and it was nothing short of compelling. Meditate and you get to study your own parade of thoughts, rather than be at the effect of them. The voices in our head can be calmed by observation, and equanimity. Meditation and focused awareness can facilitate many facets of our life, but it is also the best antidote I know for another tendency we might call spiritual restlessness. Seekers and mall strollers alike are inclined toward compulsive shopping for the next New Thing.

We tend to be collectors. We get one splendid idea from this book, we get another brilliant notion from that course. We keep ourselves busy by collecting various, shiny nuggets of wisdom, and then with our basket of notions we go over this mountain and that one and the next.

Humans like to accumulate things, including trinkets

of wisdom. Some have even given this wisdom dabbling and collecting a name: spiritual materialism.

I have read and collected some of the great books, but until I met myself in sincere practice and did the real work on my own, I kicked up a lot of colorful dust, but I barely got any closer to the quiet depths. Intellectual understanding is important, but if that's where it stops then there can be more dust, and shadow, than light. So rather than kick up yet another storm I decided to sit. Not unlike Chaplin's Tramp, I finally sat my tired self down and examined my poor, often-stubbed toes.

So how might we refresh both our soles and our souls? How might we crush our own bones into the fine powder of self realization? We go deep. We keep at it. We wander off the path, we get back on it. We get on to the meditation cushion, get off, go about our business, and then return to the cushion. At a certain point, I knew I had to go past reading and study. There's watching a cooking show, and then there's peeling onions and potatoes in your kitchen. There's huffing and puffing through one's day, always trying to catch up with yourself, and then there's sitting still and following your breath. This work-hard, play-hard fellow finally decided to do both.

Through meditation and practice, I found, over time, I could actually refashion my own interior landscape. I could dance with that untamed bull kicking behind my eyes.

Meditation is a world dance that we undertake singularly. Yet in the very depths of our solitude we are united with the beating heart of all that lives, and to the earth, and the hammock of space that holds all the worlds. It is one place where we as individuals are fully nourished, yet it is also the one place that our individuality dies. Being

KEN TAUB

still, we catch glimpses of an ancient, timeless face.

So I sat in meditation, but in a hopeful way. At first, I actually believed it would take me Someplace Else. I thought that these depths were The New Place To Go, the ultimate destination. At last, Ken had the enlightenment approach at his disposal, and this surely had to be the right approach.

Well, yes . . . and no. Inspired, we try a new tack, one that usually does not work much better for us than the last. After the newness and eagerness waned, I came to see that there is no end point. Even with profound meditation, there is really no Oz, just as there is, ultimately, no "solution." But what may seem to be the ultimate bummer turns out to be the underlying gospel of unperturbed awareness. The no-place-to-go is the good news. Simply stated, there is no bigger, better Over There.

After enough false starts or some major difficulty in our lives, we may finally stop spinning long enough to slow down and take an honest, if exhausted, look at precisely where we are. Doing so, we begin to engage in a real practice, one where we come to realize that *the road we are currently walking on is The Path.* We have the opportunity to pay attention to what's right before us. With this approach, life becomes less about what "happens to us" than what we choose to do with what we find in front of us.

Remember the expression "finding yourself"? Well, the only time I found myself is when I found myself precisely where I was standing. Or sitting.

Not the End Point, but This Point

I wanted metaphysical momentum. I wanted earthshaking insight and unalterable transformation, and I thought a stronger meditation practice would take me *there*. I didn't quite know where *there* was, but I surely knew it wasn't *here*. Turns out, I was peaking over the horizon, looking past where I was actually standing. I had the noble goal of enlightenment in mind. The only problem with this noble aim was that I was missing the light shining on my own two feet. Today I know this: that it is possible (essential really) to enjoy the process, the small moments, the valleys as well as the peaks—in short, the entire joyous mess. We may be able to leap over a small crevasse, but we do not get to jump over time, and what's right before us. Be it painful or pleasureable, new or routine, here is this occurance—and here is our life.

Some simple examples may be in order. As noted, I have been a runner for more than half of my life, and I surely enjoy the endorphin high that comes after a good run and a good, healthy sweat. But I do not run for the endorphin high, with that forefront in mind as I jog down the street. I enjoy the stretching beforehand, the scenery of the jog, the joy of being physical, the fact that my knees and feet haven't given out on me yet, all of it. The brief, pleasant endorphin experience is just one more thing. If I lost the ability to move my legs, I would fantasize not about the runner's high afterwards but about the run itself. I would yearn for the sheer joyous physicality of it.

From here, its a simple sidestep to another perennially favorite physical activity. Orgasms are grand. But once we gain some experience in our lovemaking, isn't it equally grand to engage in long, deep kissing; creative foreplay that involves giggles as well as moans; and of course the act of intercourse itself, that delicious union which makes us brainy mammals so mindlessly happy? How much exquisite feeling do we miss if we only rush forward to the "goal line" of orgasm? Do we race past our own ever changing banquet of ecstacy for a 20 second dessert? Aren't we always looking for some payoff?

The same goes for practice. Many people, this person included, might tend to see the attainment of great clarity, or samadhi, as the goal of practice, especially in the earlier years of one's meditation work. The sensation of "dropping away of body and mind" (an apparent shift or slowing down of the reasoning and physical awareness centers of the brain's frontal lobe and parietal lobe) is undeniably an enjoyable and worthwhile experience. It can open us up to free us up.

During those intermittent moments where I would experience a profound quiet and a greater opening, I would usually think in the immediate aftermath something like: "This is it! Here is the ground I want to occupy." Even larger, smarter rats want to continually hit the bar that activates the pleasure center or the deep relaxation center of our mammallian brain.

However, if one only focuses primarily on achieving a state of bodiless union one may easily miss the beautiful nuances of the baking or leaf raking one is doing just prior to meditation, not to mention the moment by moment changes in breath, being and external stimuli as one is seated in meditation. Seeking, one still has a goal—*over yonder*—in mind. So I asked myself, is the greater stillness of samadhi "better than" hearing the birds' rich singing outside my window in the first ten minutes of meditation? Or are they are just different experiences?

Perhaps we sit in silence not merely for its own sake, but to better hear the music. Or, which part of our short lives do we not want to be present to?

The Difficult and the Tremendously Difficult

Paying attention and being present is something we can all do, even in the midst of great difficulty. Of course many people have extremely trying lives. Many have known a string of tragedies. For nearly every single one of us, life often feels like it is careening from the merely troubling to the tremendously difficult. Life is very hard in Africa, but life is not easy in America. Of course there are differences. We should acknowledge differences in health, opportunity, education and economics. All the same, having money doesn't often help you get clear about your life. And there are surely times when difficulty builds alertness and compassion, as well as character.

That said, this fortunate boy from the suburbs had an early interest in the Big Questions and in Buddhism. The ancient winds whispered in a receptive ear. It is called boddhicitta in Buddhism, the awakened heart, and while some will point to a certain kind of spiritual acumen or even to reincarnation, most Buddhists and my own experience state that it is something that we all have in one degree or another. It is obvious that there are those with innate mathematical or musical ability, that there are people born with great athletic potential or simply more grace than the majority of persons, but the awakened heart is something different. No matter how many hours I practiced, I could not compose music like Mozart or shoot hoops like Michael Jordan.

Not so with waking up. The beautiful paradox of the awakened heart is this: we all have it, it usually lies partially shrouded or temporarily locked tight, but it is always there, not unlike the sun behind thick clouds. The world has opened before us because we have opened up to the world. Eden is no longer myth, and we are no longer banished from it. Here it is, and here we are in it.

Now please know this: it is easy to say what I just said above. Sure, this is *this*. We are all One. Wake up and the world wakes up with you. Choose your favorite timeless catch phrase. But before we know Unity we know this: Pain. Everyone but everyone I know has experienced the pain of loss, the pain of loneliness, the pain of isolation, confusion and despair. Too many have experienced the pain of war, hunger, poverty or civil unrest. And we have all known some form of scorn or rejection, the pain of physical agony and of illness, and the sheer pain of being an individual being. I have even heard people complain at vacation health spas. Suffering is everywhere.

Surely, we bring a great deal of misery upon ourselves and those around us, but we did not create mass plagues or Sudden Infant Death Syndrome, earthquakes or floods, old age or arthritis. It is a well-intentioned but deceptive New Age sentiment to believe that there is really only Love and Light in this life and that pain is only spiritual constipation. To a large extent, this life is very much about suffering and pain.

In fact, it would not be unfair to say that pain is the central axis around which the human condition revolves. Here is where an honest spiritual practice must start. Our foundation and so our quest may be for love, peace and serenity, but we look for these things largely because they tend to appear so infrequently, while pain and loss is around us at all times, or just around the corner. Pay Great Pain its due, it is not to be denied. This is our condition.

Enter The Dragon

So we come to real practice: the courage and presence of mind to shake hands with pain, and the control and maturity to be inwardly still even amidst all the exciting distractions. Being deeply still through seated meditation is not a mini-vacation. It is sitting down with our very lives. It is being without commenting. But how do we do this?

Here is where one television-fed, sense gratifying, skeptical Westerner looks East, to someone who lived two and a half millenia before our time. There is a unique trail-blazer here, a person who tunneled so deeply into the nature of human suffering—indeed the nature of reality itself—that he came out, as it were, on the other shore.

This former prince from northern India decided to throw it all up in the air, and challenge every belief, supposition, tradition, cultural endowment, and established view he ever held. He did the profoundly difficult work that is necessary to go from fearful monkey mind to fearless dragon mind. Here was an overindulged child who decided, surprisingly, to become a dedicated yogi, and he did not relent until he reached his goal of ultimate repose, and a direct knowing of things *as they are*.

Upon his enlightenment, the Buddha's initial pronouncement, his first great Noble Truth, was simply this: affliction and dissatisfaction are universal, that to be alive is to suffer.

This was not an original insight. But then the Buddha, The One Who Woke Up, went on to explain why we suffer so often and so very deeply, and how we can eliminate the great majority of our suffering.

In a nutshell, we suffer because of our greed and disconnectedness. We suffer because we humans have a great tendency to grasp and hold, and less of one to release and let go. We tend to cling, and we are most often dissatisfied with whatever comes our way, either right off the bat or over time. We also suffer because of the very way we view ourselves.

Like almost everyone I have ever met, I too was un-questionably talented at becoming quickly dissatisfied with nearly everything I'd ever done and with fully everything I had ever possessed. We are greedy monkeys, we want what we don't have, and we often share with great reluctance. To this day, the overall human condition is essentially the same as it was 250 or 2,500 years ago; there is enough for everyone but some have too much while the majority have too little. It is as if we believe that scarcity is still the norm and bounty is rare. As such, we persistently convince ourselves we can armor our bodies or amass enough stuff to keep death, pain and "dreaded other" forever at bay.

There are times that modern civilization behaves more civilly. Certain societies are better today at "distrib-uting the wealth" than were the pharaohs, kings and war-lords of old, but whether we look at the local picture or the global picture, every single one of us knows in the deepest chambers of our hearts that with the right amount of effort and attention nearly everyone could prosper. We tend to behave this way during times of natural disaster and in the aftermath of human brutality, so we know we are capable of it. But when the floodwaters recede and the victims are treated, we quickly go back to business as usual. Why is that?

It is not because we are secretly mean at heart, it is be-cause of a sadly unwholesome perspective, and subse-quent wrong-thinking. We think of ourselves and others as separate, and endlessly competing for the earth's bounty. We also see the rest of the world, both animals and other peoples, as "outside, over there." It is one of the more tragic consequences of not knowing who or what we really are.

But there is something even deeper than our clinging and hoarding, or our ancient fear of beasts and strangers. We also suffer more than is necessary because we resist suffering, or that which we label as suffering. It sounds strange, because surely it makes a kind of sense to avoid suffering, does it not? Seeking comfort or warmth or food or affection does not make us bad, it only makes us human. Oddly enough, the problem comes when we call what comes our way a problem.

There are things which we prefer, and there are things we label either good or bad. Like most, I railed against that which made me uncomfortable or that which I feared might harm me, not unlike Captain Ahab fending off Moby Dick. But what happened to Ahab? He got entangled in his own harpoon lines and became one with his perceived menace. I can tell you this: I have surely been Ahab in my life.

I have been the one that got in my own way the most.

But are we just to accept everything that comes our way, and smile? Did this Indian philosopher and doctor of the mind instruct his followers to forsake personal struggle and to remain passive instead? No, precisely the opposite. The Buddha did not much concern himself with the origin of the universe or whether there is an afterlife. Nor did the Buddha tell people to hide from obstacles, the sharp edges of human relationships, or life's larger hardships. He did more than sit serenely. He stood firm.

The Buddha made a living declaration for us to be present, to be mindful, to remain awake, and not wish for sunshine in the middle of a fierce rainstorm or to drift off into fantasy after being bit by a scorpion. We acknowledge the rain and the pain, we don't need to pretend it's not there or to use all our energy to immediately push it away. We're aware that the hurt hurts; we go with it, we stay present to it, and then we seek shelter from the storm and medical attention for our maladies, scorpion venom included.

To be genuinely awake in this life is to create a rolling, unfenced field—a vastly larger context—which does not eliminate fear, pain and suffering, but rather holds it in such a way that it is diminished not magnified, engaged not shunned as Other, and, *after a good amount of practice*, is seen as naught but a passing shower, an occurrence that happens to be in front us. The event is the same, the discomfort is real or the menace is real, but one person grabs the bulls by the horns while the other is a graceful toreador. One fights while the other dances.

Retraining the Ninny

Awake to the moment, one also learns to let go. Take everyday traffic, as an example. Two people are stuck in a long traffic jam. The person in the first car is cursing and slamming his steering wheel in anger and resentment. The person in the car right behind the angry driver also has somewhere she has to be, also is no fan of traffic jams, but rather than "spit into the wind," she quickly acknowledges that this is simply the prevailing circumstance, not a private punishment. So she exhales, settles into the moment and goes with the flow, even when the flow is temporarily bottled up.

You know how we can sometimes sit with serene detachment as we carefully pry a splinter from our foot? It is possible to extend that kind of attentive care to a whole host of painful and uncomfortable situations, including things that hurt us a great deal. Over time, we are able to train our reflexive minds. With meditation practice we are, in one sense, retraining that forever distraught ninny within us. Yet there is something that happens that is even greater than *the diminishment of suffering by a radical change in perspective.*

Continued practice—ongoing meditation and mindful living—can eventually eliminate most of the walls that separate us from other people, other cultures, other species, and even the unknown. Now, the moment I utter a foolish remark about someone or some group, I can feel the sting of disingenuousness there, and the boomerang heading straight back at the thrower. What's *really* going on is not on the outside. The problem is not "them." The power of meditation and mindfulness training is that it tends by its nature to replace that protective persona that gets up with us first thing in the morning. Pretense and protection are replaced by presence. There is now a real beauty before us in the early morning bathroom mirror, one that will not fade with time.

Convenient Fictions

Ongoing mindfulness practice is like slow erosion; bit by bit it washes over and dilutes the ego that reacts or defends with a liquid self which *embraces all that it encounters.* Not a well-intentioned hug, mind you, for all that is violent, wild and dangerous, but rather a more oceanic acceptance; the begining of the end to all the fences that require endless mending, and a dissolution of the made-up borders—both geographic and interpersonal—that we have become so bloody used to we believe they are real. Over time, I could finally see the falsehoods I had created, and know that they were only convenient fictions.

When we are able to let go our man-made fences, let stress and pain be stress and pain, and let go of our end of the rope, then a profound shift is possible. Once we slow down, stop protecting what need not be protected, or stop wincing in fear and resistance, pain, stress, and even sadness tend to dissolve into minor discomfort . . . then a distinct physical sensation . . . then a few deep breaths . . . and then nothing much of anything.

Now keep it mind that this work is called a "practice" because we have to keep at it, not unlike exercise. Letting go takes continual practice, and even after one has years of meditation retreats under their belt, the mind is quick to go back to longing, self importance, self pity, a wish for things to be the way we want them, and a whole host of other attachments. I could personally testify in court to this.

The good news is that we can keep our weight down by exercise and keep sober with support groups. And we can overcome our little dramas with Big Mind.

The great sage from India showed, through teaching and example, the way to gain insight into our reflexive behaviors and delusions so that we might go on to cultivate mindfulness. Mindfulness gives us access to new possibilities. Nearly everything becomes interesting and novel, while nearly every place becomes as compelling as Maui simply because it is.

Quiet, clear seeing is also a passageway that leads to radical empathy, otherwise known as compassion. Boundaries start to dissolve. After all, sharing and support are natural. We are a highly social species, and very much a part of the ecosystems we inhabit. Other is not really other. Any shells we create are just that: created, artificial. They are real in one sense, yet they are far less real than the flow of life.

The Buddha demonstrated with his own life that we can open up more than we might have even dared imagine. We can break through our shells, and grow. We can stop picking on ourselves, and dwelling in regret and recrimination. We can live life without reliance on television, endless electronic noise and other forms of doping, without the latest fads we snicker at and then indulge in, and we can do without many more things. We can even give up the oddly comforting crutch of our neuroses. We can in fact subdue and transform our fearful monkey minds. It just takes work.

Here is what helped hook this fish: I found out that it was possible to be more than a slave of my senses, but to completely occupy my senses—to fully taste the fresh fruit I was eating, and to actually be *of* the beach when I was fortunate enough to be on the beach. I began to occupy, and profoundly love, this very physical body.

Paradoxically, by being still enough often enough, I was able to appreciate the runner and the running. I slowly began to sit deeply enough that I could shake the many selves off of myself, not unlike a furry old dog getting water off its body. I actually got to sit quietly, below the surface. Masks were disgarded, personal myths were pierced. It was not magic, nor was it terribly difficult.

The transformation of personal suffering into the kind of open-ended clarity that comes from paying attention and being present is a continual process. Our entire lives are the process. Each moment of our life is It. The pleasant moments, the stressful moments, the ecstatic moments, the sad moments, we work with them all. Eventually, it is possible for every kind of wood—even the pieces that are nearly petrified, or those with thorns, the pieces that can cause us pain—to be kindling for our fire. And the fire of an awakened being rejects nothing, consumes everything, and so burns with an exquisite brightness.

4

Hot Tub Zen

THE MAXIMUM DELICIOUS TUMULT *of all creation filled the space in between their physical love, and their sweat, and all their rising-falling dream breaths, and with the wild he of it and the wild she of it, and all of it, and then none of it, they rose up and embraced before descending into dust and the light dancing in between the particles of dust, and then back into the warm earth.*

She shifted her torso on the soft, white sheets. She said, "I love the way you touch me. And I love the way you move."

He studied the very tip of her nose, and smiled. He enjoyed nothing more than studying her good face, from her smooth, caramel skin, to her wide brow, to the tip of her intelligent nose.

She took in his complete attention, his intoxicated focus, and smiled from within, almost audibly, not unlike the deep coo of a pigeon. She leaned over, kissed him. He felt the rustle once again, and wrapped his right arm around her side, placing his right hand on the center of her spine. Immediately, they were kissing deep, and they took off yet again.

They rose and fell, rose and fell; rose until there was not any high place to go, fell until there was no more down place anywhere. He grabbed both of her hands, they interlaced all their fingers, and raised all four arms above their heads. They kissed hard again, crushing themselves together until they were gone and forgotten and away from all their homes and fences, fortresses and moats. They were gone from all of it, including themselves, and deep they went into this departure, swinging away and back, one into another, one into no one, gone, together, until it all went bright white, then pitch black, and then everything.

Right off the bat, it is a fair question to ask: why all this focus on pain and suffering? Sure, there is a lot of suffering in this world, but isn't there a great deal of pleasure too? Haven't any of these devout people ever gone to a tailgate party or to the South Beach portion of Miami? What is it with most religions, Buddhism and Zen included, that they are drawn to the flames of suffering like grim moths? It is a good and worthwhile question. Yes, there is the life-affirming party that is an Irish wake, the dancing Hasidic Jews, the dazzling Sufi Whirling Dervishes, the joyous noise of a loud African-American Gospel choir, and a few remaining pagan rituals of the earthy sort, but for the most part there is an incessant, depressing focus on the dark side, the downside, and of course, everyone's favorite breakfast topic, death.

In the yin and yang perspective, isn't there a flip side to Life is Suffering? How about Life is Bliss? The answer is of course yes. If we intend on being even mildly optimistic and occasionally joyous then we have to look at the larger donut, not just at the hole. After all, if Zen and Buddhism are so concerned about being present, and thus more fully living our lives, why not pay equal attention to romping in the ocean, pick-up basketball, comedy and laughter, that ice cream cone dripping down one's arm, or that naked body right before us? Why not indeed.

We all know about the fear and mistrust our ancient Judeo-Christian forefathers had about pleasure and the earthly delights. The Muslims were just as resistant, and some are even more fearful of the body, especially the female body. Many of the Hindus and Taoists were a little less puritanical, but there are also many dour Hindus who frown on Eros and the playful side of life. As for Buddhism, most early Buddhists were monks who refrained from playing around, and it is only when the Buddha's dharma traveled to China (around the year 500) and met up with some of those free-wheeling country Taoists that Zen was born, eastern moonshine was introduced, and lounging on the hillside staring at the clouds was encouraged. Buddhism and Ch'an (meditation) then moved on to Korea and Japan where it became the Zen we are most familiar with. In Japan, it also became largely austere, somewhat martial or militant, quite ceremonial, and very, very male. It had lost some of its Yin, or soft side, and the vast majority of Zen Buddhists were men for hundreds of years.

Today Buddhism and Zen are in Europe and America, and you can count on this: some of the lighter side of life will be reintroduced into the enlightenment culture.

You can get Americans or Europeans up at four in the morning to do zazen, but when the the day or week of focused meditation is over, count on a lot of noisy dining and no small amount of partying. We are a culture more inclined to living with gusto like Zorba the Greek, and not like humble monks. Frankly, I think this will do all forms of Buddhism a world of good. Many of the sects, Zen included, needed a good, fresh breeze. Besides, I'd much rather hang with people who enjoy, and share, their chocolate, and who like getting into the hot tub once invited.

Of perhaps greater importance is the fact that a lot of Western Zen students and teachers are women, and more than our infectious enthusiasm, openness and playfulness, it will be the role of women which will surely change both the face of Buddhism in the West as well as the very path toward self-realization and awakening. I believe this can not be overstated. There were very few women like Charlotte Joko Beck in Japan's old Zen societies, and few figures like Pema Chodron in Tibet (p.s., in my view, their books are very much worth reading). Their earthy influence, tendency toward loving kindness, feminine perspective, as well as their deep practice and fierce determination will take us into uncharted territory, and I believe it will be an excellent, well lit landscape.

Women excel at bringing us down to earth and back into our bodies. Women, I find, are also more inclined toward inclusiveness and less likely to be regimented. Therefore the many thousands of female practitioners (some sanghas and Buddhist centers in America have more women than men), and dozens of female teachers, will change not only what it is to be a Buddhist in the West, but even what it means to be an enlightened being. Surely, they will redefine the meaning of enlightened culture.

But back to the hot tub, please. Can one really be a mindful hedonist? Can one be fully of this world and an open hearted, empty handed bodhisattva too? Isn't the desire for sex and pleasure one of the biggest deterrents to prudent and simple living, not to mention a major, kaleidoscopic distraction?

Not in my view. Sexuality is the racing pulse of existence, the warm wellspring of life. Sexual love is not just a human trait, it is a universal current. It is hardly an accident that Divine Nature has made our sexual experiences so enjoyable. First we tingle and then we arch toward transcendence, eyes closed in a waking dream, mouth open in bliss. Our sexuality too is divine, and the healthy expression of it is inherently joyous and expansive. It not only involves a potential act of creation—the procreation of our species—it is also the quintessential act of Creation itself: unifying, radiant, giving, yielding, achingly pleasurable, carnal, magnificent.

It is no surprise to me that all of the established Zen teachers that I have studied with are sexual beings. Many are married (some several times), they like to have a roll in the hay as well as a hardy laugh, and a trip into the city along with a hike in the wilderness. Some own cars, like a good belt of fermented grain now and again, and they even go to nightclubs. Has any of this detracted from their practice or their wisdom? No, just the opposite. Do I ever wish that I had left worldliness behind me and studied in a cave, a forest or a monastery for five years in order to expedite my fuller awakening? Never.

Give up sex, chocolate, sports, dancing, the gym, a jog on the beach and HBO? Why? Really now, what would be the point? Life is short enough, thank you.

It may work for some to get out of the fray and to leave relationships and prior attachments behind for a time in order to focus solely on one's self realization. There is value to this approach. Yet there is also value in waking up to our lives *as they are* and not "home leaving." After all, do we get away from the mundane and our everyday routine to run away, or to go deeper?

Yes, we are better off for keeping up our spiritual practice. Of course, we can not eat whatever we want, whenever we want, and remain trim and fit. Nor can we indulge every whim and satisfy every urge and remain mindful and clear. Everything worthwhile requires discipline and giving up several small things so we can accomplish the more crucial Big Thing (or the Tremendous No-thing, if you prefer).

Can it be more of a struggle or a lengthier process to alter one's perspective and to clarify one's vision while at home, at work and with the family? You bet. But it can be done, and besides, after we wake up, we almost always return to the relationships, the unfinished business, the tumult and the distractions, both pleasant and painful, that we left behind. In fact, if we do not return to our loved ones and to the world, then what is our realization really about? Do we wake up to sit on a mountain top, humming to ourselves until we pass away? Or do we go back into our families and into the bustle, the entanglements, and the noisy, messy marketplace of life to live it even more fully and to make a difference in the lives of others? For me, the choice is clear. It is also the choice of a fully realized Bodhisattva, the most compassionate social workers of the cosmos.

I also believe that a more enlightened society will not shun Eros and human sexuality, but rather celebrate it in positive and meaningful ways. Increasingly, in the West and many other parts of the world, we are leaving the shame behind and entering the more sublime aspects of erotic play and a healthier sexual liberation.

Let us indulge in a pleasant diversion. Imagine this 21st century scenario of perhaps only twenty, thirty or forty years from now . . . Here we see worldly and patient women in their thirties and forties teaching younger women about the art of making love, and initiating eager young men into the sublime world of erotic pleasure. Friends, both singles and couples, make dates to share once esoteric, taboo sexual techniques, and then demonstrate what they know on one another with no games, no guilt, and all of it being no big deal. Physical pleasure has been stolen away from the cruel, ancient regime of secrecy and guilt and transformed into a brand new realm of playfulness and acceptance. People are still not making love on the street, but women friends get together to offer advise and support—sometimes hands on—on how to relax and reach new peaks of pleasure. Men speak to one another about techniques that drive women to ecstacy, and talk more openly about the problems they are having in the bedroom with the ease they used to display talking to one another about their golf swing. Secret shame has been replaced by real support. More adults join the very youngest of our tribe in a carefree, naked romp on the beach, splashing happily in the warm waters in our God-given birthday suits. Sex is actually considered good for one's health, and treated more often as a long, sumptuous meal rather than as fast food, or worse, junk food, Sexual education classes in school are thorough, scientific and enthusiastically supported by parents. Surburban neighborhoods have the now standard yoga centers and Tantric yoga classes too, showing participants how the physical can also lead to intimitate contact with the Divine.

Contraceptives are not taboo but topics of intelligent discussion. Accordingly, teen pregnancy is down dramatically from the bad old days of the 20th century. There is also no prostitution as we know it today. Courtesans and surrogates are professionally licensed and trained—just like massage and physical therapists are today—and work solely to enhance pleasure and to offer relief and release to servicemen, older men, men going through separation or divorce, and to many different men for many different reasons, as opposed to operating pathetically, stressfully and illegally in dark corners and dingy hotel rooms. In this sane place, women can and do go to erotic masseurs for their choice of full body massage or full body orgasm. It has become quite well accepted that when men are away, or selfish, or are simply not available, women may please themselves, and each other. It is also widely understood that the original "love chemicals" that once enlivened our brains when the relationship was new fade after two to four years (not to mention after two, four or more children), and so couples can head to a Lover's Enhancement Center for a private or group refresher course in making sex lively, explorative, and red hot once again. People accept that it takes work to stay in "erotic shape" after a few years together or after a certain age, and so they do something about it. Sex, which was always important to the human species, is finally being treated as the meaningful, positive, compelling, varied, healthy, and yes, spiritually powerful force that it is.

Personally, I wish such a future on my son and all the young people of the world. And while upcoming sexual possibilities may seem like an unlikely diversion for a book on transcending our messes and achieving self realization, I think it is an unavoidable topic when we are talking about Buddhism in the West, mindful living in the 21st century, and what a realistic, full-blooded, fully human, enlightened society might look like. Simply stated, waking up must absolutely encompass all corners of our lives, from our jobs, to the raising of our children and what they are taught in school, to how we brush our teeth and take care of our bodies, fornication very much included. Anything left out is not whole, anything not whole is not fully integrated, nor is it full enlightenment.

I sense that the future just described is already beginning to happen, and I believe that this is the sexual future we may likely see. Some may find it excessive or even distasteful, but if it is to be a truly healthy sexual future, then one will have a choice to partake or to simply say no thank you, and go for or a walk or plant in the garden.

In this picture I have painted will there likely be some excess and cruel behavior? Yes, when you have human beings involved in just about anything you have selfishness, and unnecessary pain inflicted. There is malicious behavior within the confines of home and marriage, and there will be some here too, even in a more sexually healthy world. That said, I would prefer to live in our sexual world than in the sexual world of the Middle Ages or Victorian England, and I think that there will continue to be more effective education and less blind fear about human sexuality, so that our children's sexual future will be a more mature, healthier, happier one. There has been evolution in the past few generations, and there is still much room for improvement, and greater sexual sanity.

We all have different upbringings, tastes and proclivities. My own upbringing—the time, the place, and my parents especially—made it a virtual certainty that I would wind up being free-spirited, not repressed. I had down-to-earth, sexy folks and grew up in sexually experimental times. Sex for me is something that is natural, positive and life-affirming, not to mention wildly pleasurable. I do not shy away from Eros, I embrace it. So it is no surprise that my instincts and my own life experience have taught me to shy away from and be very wary of those who speak ill of sexuality, as well as adult play, idle curiosity, the scientific method, democracy, human rights, rock n' roll, and driving down that long stretch of highway for no particular reason and with no particular place to go.

The freedom to be who we are, to live life unfettered by the authorities and so rich with liberty, is not only the life I know, but the life I think almost everyone on this planet wisely desires. Of course there are valid ways to live one's life and construct the social contract other than the American way and Western-style democracy, but there is still no substitute for political freedom and personal liberty. What person, or culture, is not better off free?

It is also a very good thing that there are monks, mystics and ascetics in the world. Hot sex or frequent club-hopping are not yet spiritual requirements. Surely, it is good that there are people who place pleasure and possessions well behind charity, chastity and the conscious, committed poverty of renunciation for the wealth of a deeper faith. Our world is a better place because there are such spiritually committed people living in it.

That said, I acknowledge the culture and times that formed me, and I acknowledge my own proclivities and life choices. Thus, I enthusiastically throw my body into the favorable circle of Eros, my hat in the ring of freedom, and bow to the artists and iconoclasts, and those who wrote the Constitution and The Bill of Rights. I bow to da Vinci and Henry Miller, to Thomas Jefferson and Ben Franklin, as well as to Buddha.

5

Terra Firma

IF THERE IS WHOLESALE REINCARNATION, I want to come back here. I love the earth. Find me in a large open space, on a wide stretch of beach, in the center of the ocean's circle, on a rocky mesa, or any place where there is naught but patch and sky and where wildness reigns, and my heart expands to fill that space. I have a love affair with this planet.

While I am not always proud of what we human beings have done, I am always proud to call myself an earthling, and to be one of the lucky critters living atop this massive, molten-cored, thickly forrested, oceanic cell. It is a grand place, and when I am fortunate enough to be out in wide spaces or wild places, I rarely fail to see Paradise before me. Most days, I see plenty that is paradisaical in my own backyard. Now what this means to my own practice and to my digestion of the Buddha's dharma is that I have no real concerns about Nirvana, any more than I have about inhabiting a medieval interpretation of Heaven in the clouds. My focus is on the space and the landscape before me. Nirvana here or Nirvana down the road, it makes no nevermind to me.

The next adventure will be the next adventure, whether it turns out to be Profound Silence, some form of spirit recycling, or a higher, lighter sphere of being. My resources only tell me that the scouting reports vary a great deal about what's to come once we finish with our present bodies. So I am content to find out when I find out, and to relish the big surprise. Even Buddha did not speak with finality about an afterlife, either because he too did not know what was to come, or he saw no benefit to his disciples living a more wholesome, productive, generous life on earth by spilling the beans. Personally, I believe it was the first reason, but no matter.

There is a point to this of course, and I think it is an important one. It is about fully occupying and indeed loving the ground one stands upon this moment, or the meditation cushion one sits upon, whether it is in a corner of a messy room or in a monastery in the mountains. It is about appreciating one's home, one's town, one's nation and one's planet. Remain convinced that life will be better only after you move to San Diego or Stockholm, or that existence will be vastly improved the moment *after* one takes one's last breath, and one not only gambles on the magic longshot, one also misses the countless miracles right under one's nose every blessed day.

So my own heartfelt notion of waking up is not some smooth, friction-free ideal of enlightened life over yonder, but rather waking up to my own life, my own wife and child, my own home, my hometown, to America the beautiful, and to this tremendously breathtaking and breath-giving planet.

To the extent that I remain appreciative and humbly grateful for all I have—especially this very life and this living moment—is the extent that I am present and accounted for. This person here only has one shot at living in this bag of skin and going on this particular adventure; he only has one shot at this day; he sees this very sight once and only once, even in his well studied backyard.

I have been known to voice a complaint or two in my time, but the moment I stop my tongue from flapping, or sit upon the cushion, or take a breath and look carefully about me to view our amazing world, I am more grateful for this life than I can ever put into words. This gratitude rests peaceably in the deepest chambers of the man's being, and it grows with each passing year.

An earthy enlightenment is about relishing that great meal, or that single slice of bread. But it is more than that. It is about getting fresh soil beneath one's fingernails. But it is more than that. It is about having a good run, and fully experiencing the good air filling one's lungs. But it is more than that too. It is about the miracle of life, right here . . . the forever folding and unfolding enigma . . . the part cloudy, part clear sky of existence . . . the in and out of breath and being . . . . . This!

An earthy enlightenment is being enlightened by life's grand parade, what the Chinese call the 10,000 Things. We wake up, arise from our slumber and remeet the multitude of phenomena and colorful appearances before us, the spectacular kaleidoscope of life.

An earthy enlightenment is fully appreciating this earth, as noted, but it is all the more about seeing one's self as earth. Our environment is no longer a "natural amusement park" for us to stomp upon like thoughtless children, our environment is who we are. It is more than our proto-parent; it's nature is our nature. Its integrity is our own.

There is a sacredness to this place. We walk on holy ground. Everywhere.

City streets and national parks are holy. The Amazon and the Antarctic, equally holy. The dirt path or the highway can be holy. My backyard is holy. Then so is the dog whimpering to go out at 11:45 at night, followed by the babe crying at 2:22 a.m. That too is holy. The fall leaves falling, the blinding snowstorm. Holy, holy. The fire raging in the forest and that long stretch of the super green 17th fairway. Both holy. The first cup of coffee in the straining morning light or the four-course dinner at sunset. Holy squared. The island of Manhattan and the island of Kauai. One is thoroughly drenched in holiness, yet the other is too. The derelict sitting in his own urine in a dark alley and my child romping in the flowered field. Both are pitiful, wonderful, searingly poignant, fleeting expressions of holiness.

It's all holy. The whole earth is holy. Thank God.

58

6

The Enlightenment Bugaboo
(and other traps)

I HAVE NOT MET A single person yet who spent a great deal of time on their meditation cushion because it was just too cold outside to do anything else, or because there was nothing good on cable. Every practitioner I ever met—whether they chose to travel far into the forests of Thailand, or a few hundred miles to a Zen Center, or simply retreat to a corner of their bedroom—all had one immense goal in mind. Attaining enlightenment.

When we start our quest the majority of us have a few loose, romantic notions about enlightenment, while most of the time we have a hard time describing what it is, exactly, or why we even want to pursue it. But no matter, we want it just the same. Perhaps it is our own exotic, lofty notion of enlightenment that beckons us. We are clearly in love with the *idea* of it.

KEN TAUB

I remember returning to New York in the late 1970s, at the height of the disco era, when seemingly every fourth person was dying to get into Studio 54. They had only heard about the place, they had not seen it for themselves, they likely would not be allowed in (it was, after all, a place for *special* people), but those prohibitions only served to whet their appetite. *"I hear it's great! I want in!"*

Enlightenment is not unlike Studio 54. For the neophyte, it is the ultimate place to be. It's something we believe we do not have, so . . . we want it. In fact the verb most often attached to enlightenment is attain. She *attained* enlightenment. He went off to India on a spiritual pilgrimage. He wanted to *attain* enlightenment. *"Excuse me, I'll have a quart of milk, a loaf of whole wheat, a box of tissues, and some enlightenment please."*

In fact, enlightenment is more like gravity. For most of us, from grade school child on up to physics major, gravity manifests itself as a concept, when it fact gravity is all around us. Without this omnipresent force, we'd be something else. Or we'd be nowhere.

The radical truth about the enlightened state is not much more than a frog on a log . . . or a dirty windshield that only needs a quick rinse (or not) . . . or a mother cuddling her babe . . . or a first timer gliding down through the clouds on his initial parachute jump . . . or the walker, simply walking.

The street rap tends to go along these lines: meditate and chant, practice long and hard, struggle your ass off, and you'll achieve this advanced state of being. As such, we are inclined to see Enlightenment as something *over there*, or in Herculian terms, as a state of bliss attained by an elite few. However we conceptualize it, most of us are damn sure of one thing: we ain't got it.*"That person may have it, but I sure don't,"* we mutter to ourselves in a million ways as we stumble down the street, and stumble through our lives.

The reality is that we are, in absolute terms, frogs on the log. We are all babes in arms, wrapped in a vast, unending bosom, seen and unseen. We are not endlessly inept, we are quite capable of clearing off our dirty visors. We are all spinning through space, hitched to the earth, which is us. We are innately beautiful gravity surfers. And our eyes are meant to be open during this fantastic ride.

The Buddha insisted, time and again, that the awakened state was a natural state, imminently accessible; that it was within our reach, intuitive, organic. To be sure, the Buddha spent years—long, difficult years—struggling with his conditioned mind, and the deep, visceral entanglement with doubt, fear and aversion. He, and thousands who followed over the past 25 centuries, worked enormously hard to see through and finally rest easy with the great human tendency to grasp, cling, and think mostly about ourselves. There was no one snap insight. Forget the legends, none of this came overnight.

That said, if we infuse our practice with just two ounces of optimism, and add a relaxation of the muscles of cynicism, together this might create an easier, almost carefree receptiveness. Doing so, we will not only be exhibiting a wonderful Beginner's Mind, we will, in essence, be starting at the "end point." Sure, we will still have to put in determined, consistent effort to operate outside our reflexive, conditioned behaviors, but we will not have to be struggling painfully every step of the way. (Picture this: you're swimming in a patch of warm, clear ocean, but you've been swimming hard against the current. Suddenly, you decide to stop swimming, you exhale all your air and sink softly to the gently sloping ocean floor ten feet below. Relaxed, you look up from the quiet depths and watch the ripples of activity, the choppy waves and cross-currents on the surface of the water. Seated quietly on the ocean floor, under the surface, you are able to observe the ceaseless activity in a detached, free, noiseless way. Your heart says to your head, "Oh, look at all that churning. How interesting. Look how it's no big deal, really. It's simply moving.")

Beginner's mind is open, and largely free of clutter. It temporarily suspends the judgment machine and the running commentary. It is at once private space and Big Space—without the intermittent meteor showers of opinion. We are literally in process, as in becoming. We are swimming in the water, not in our heads.

I am no advanced being. In fact, the longer I live, the more I experience myself as a primitive male, and not, for example, a mystic or a Zen adept. Or to say it another way, if we are all buddhas in disguise, then my disguise is thick, furry and base. My behaviors, like the scant but powerful human instincts we all exhibit, are largely ingrained. In certain ways—and in my own view, not just my wife's—I am hopeless. Zen meditation has not given me a personality transplant, any more than stretching my being through cosmic insight has made me any taller. I grunt, I hoot, I holler. But this primitive has given himself one advantage: continual access to Beginner's Mind.

With Beginner's Mind we are, and so will be, generally capable gravity surfers. We are not cast from Eden, we are spinning upon it. We are not looking for our galactic citizenship, we know we are born with the papers. With

Beginner's Mind, we need not endlessly yearn to fit in, to belong. As such, we begin to replace all our seeking with simple uncovering.

This state of revealing what is not really hidden is known as practice enlightenment. It is not the endless hunt for the elusive dragon of enlightenment. It is enlightenment from the get-go.

Now this is not wishful thinking, nor pretense, nor role-playing. It occurs, often in an instant, when we stop daydreaming, play acting, or playing up to an image of ourselves. It is being present and open to the possibilities of a given situation, with a minimal attachment to the outcome. It is the simple doing of a thing—be it bike riding or cutting carrots or sitting on a meditation cushion—that is largely free of self consciousness, so that the line between being and doing is no-line. And no big deal.

Goal-free wakefulness is the living embodiment of what was previously abstract enlightenment. Practice enlightenment is sitting down upon one's meditation cushion with an open heart, not an agenda. It is the being in human being. It is the absence of a walker in the walking. It is simply energy and movement, not a fixed thing, or idea. It is the scene immediately before us, the air entering our nostrils, and taking the simple, nourishing posture of seated meditation.

Yes, deep practice and on-going meditation are important . . . *but shh, just look.*

We have a choice. Go after yet another thing. Or let go. Spend years trying to attain our *idea* of enlightenment like a brass ring just inches away from the whirling carousel, or step out of constructed time and conditioned mindset (for minutes or hours, big steps or baby steps, no matter), and do something you've never done before, or do something you've done every day of your life, only differently.

We all breathe. What if we were quietly conscious of our breath, and worked with our breath, and deliberately expanded our inhalation, and then held our breath happily for just three seconds, aware of that space between inhale and exhale. And what if we did that right now . . .

Cow Pies and Sharp Teeth

I used to imagine that our daily life was like a cow pasture with piles of manure hidden nearly everywhere, and that once you entered a temple, monastery or otherwise engaged in deeper practice you could finally walk barefoot and unafraid.

I wish. Truth be told, the shit doesn't stop, and good heavens, it's everywhere. Cow pies, snares, and big metal traps with sharp teeth never go away. At best, they only disappear for a spell. Even when we know they're likely up ahead or coming in our direction, we can only strategize, deep breathe or chant our way out of just so many traps, pitfalls and piles of manure. Life remains difficult, and while we may subdue some of our fears and self-defeating notions, we do not conquer all disease, pain, conflict, chaos, carniverous beasts and humans, or death.

It is outside the scope of this book to discuss in detail the various other traps that a sincere student of the dharma and mindfulness meditation will encounter, and of course, your traps will largely be unique to you. That said, it is important to know that wrestling with one's mind—from individual history, private shame, heartache, desire, and even the hardwired portions of the human brain which we all share—can be a bruising heavyweight bout. And the deeper you go the harder it can get. Not too many people warn the uninitiated about this, and not because its such a bad "selling tool" but because everyone finds this out for himself or herself quickly enough. Simply stated, The Way is not always easy, the journey can be a hard one, and the seas of deep self inquiry will make your little boat pitch and roll. This is not one smooth sail into Nirvana. Never was, never will be. Then again, the only thing harder than the diligent practice required for self realization is no practice at all. Asleep, we keep walking into the same walls.

So where do our sincere meditative practices get us? We get to walk through the larger cow pasture with greater awareness.

Over time, we can elevate our everyday perception, and even break through our fear and doubt. Balancing the innate wholeness of practice enlightenment with consistent, focused practice, we can overcome irrational worries and fear. We find a kind of courage we might not have known we possessed, and suddenly one day we are able to sit with neither alarm nor distraction as we watch our painful pasts (and our own meddlesome minds) roll by. What happens? Bit by bit, we become our own Witness, developing a very welcome form of detachment and self acceptance.

Sit long enough and one can in fact hold almost all of it: our painful pasts, our previous errors, even some of our larger terrors. We forgive ourselves a bit more, we react to our conditioning a little less. As we sit in stillness we are able to grow. We grow into our hearts, we grow as people.

No Particular Place To Go

There is a multi-forked and crooked trail that we clear

and then set out upon. This trail has its own energies, colors, flavors, and spirit. It is a singular journey that has it's own set of charges and consequences. It is what most of us call: My Life.

My Life? While I've often had a rollicking good time, I too have had to pay a price for my attention to pleasure first, and being one perpetually bent toward the realm of the senses. Few people want to leave the amusement park when there's yet more fun to be had. While enjoying the realm of the senses, I spent less time subduing my endless desires and ill-conceived mental constructs. The price? For me, the fast lane became the slow road to waking up and quieting down.

However, the Gospel of American Playfulness does not only have a selfish side, it does contain a bright, glowing center. There is indeed Good News for the modern pleasure seeker and adventurer. We too have the opportunity for greater depth. Being a mindful hedonist means that one occupies one's body, one's senses, and one's feelings. It means that you are here, in this moment, in this place, with no urge to run off for the sake of running off. It is a deeply grounded feeling of having no particular place to go. I'm fine thanks, right here, with this.

This kind of earthiness is not indulging in pleasure to cover up our pain, like shiny paint on a rotted fence. It is indulging in pleasure, play, voyage and encounter for their own sake, and to live life with fullness. Fully entering and occupying one's senses and feelings is nothing short of a courageous act.

It is not very difficult to get inebriated and to sleep with a stranger in the dark. But actually feeling one's feelings, kissing so deeply that one becomes supremely intoxicated, crying with joy, or deep eye contact with another can often take more courage than we might care to admit. Drugs, alcohol, repetitive pornography, and endless diversions tend to close us up. Heartfelt pleasures, natural pleasures, conscious pleasures open us up, make us more tender and available, and enhance our lives. Almost every adult knows when we are engaging in something that is healthy and life-affirming, or when we are escaping from the mundane, or our deeper fears. A mindful hedonist has his or her focus on the texture and sweet coldness of the ice cream cone they are eatting. They are actually looking at the person they are speaking to. Awake, a walk in the woods actually becomes a walk in the woods. However, for most of us, we have to traverse the mindfield of our psyches to get to a place of greater ease and openness.

Here is where meditation really helps. The Buddhists denote meditation and other acts that cut through the clutter and get us back to the real and the immediate as "skillful means." There is more interest in what is productive or counterproductive than what is so-called sinful or not sinful.

Now, meditation is not always easy, and it can take us a while to quiet the mind. Before I got my little skull circus to quiet down, I would notice I was somewhat uncomfortable, even a bit rattled, as more than a few dark memories floated to the surface. I chastised myself: 'This is not supposed to be what meditation is all about!' Needless to say, this preliminary dance of fear and reluctance continues to pop up from time to time, for obvious reasons and for reasons I can not quite figure. But today, deep in the bones that support my skull, I know this: before there is peace of mind there is raking the mud of mind. It's just part of the process. And it's just noise.

Over time, we are able to get less caught up in our own messy sideshows. Simply put, we get wise to the perpetuation of our own unnecessary nonsense. We get tired of the hindrances and diversions, because they are no longer seen by the mind as safe touchstones. They are seen for what they really are: a big chunk of fool's gold, as in a blockage to a bigger freedom road.

The Wisdom of the West

For many new devotees of a chosen path, and for those who are at a crossroads in their spiritual practice, there may arise a strong temptation to push away nearly everything. There are those who adopt a posture of negation. There can even be a nearly wholesale rejection of the tasty fruits of Western science, commerce and technology, and those who would smear the deservedly lovely reputation of pleasure and comfort in the name of some idealized piety. Some even chooose to become psuedo-Tibetans or psuedo-Asian monks, hoping that a new identity will help erase the old one. We feel compelled to look for new routes back to ourselves.

While a new path and new patterns may contain many skillful elements, and while the effort in and of itself it is worthy, and while one has to shut off the CD, the computer and the car engine now and again in order to be still, and to delve deeper than our everyday hectic life tends to take us, one does not become enlightened by trading in pop music or sunny days on the beach for a robe, a gong and a black cushion. Knowing this up front can possibly save one a lot of time and undue heartache.

India has provided the rest of us with yoga and Buddhism. Japan refined and distilled Buddhism into the brilliantly precise and potent Zen we know today. There is a great deal to be learned by looking back, and looking to the East. There is surely nothing wrong with going to India, Thailand, Burma or Japan to study. They have much to teach us.

However, we are not lacking on this side of the globe. Need we trample on our Western culture and history, suddenly finding fault with it at nearly every turn? Perhaps, with a fuller, more mature perspective, we can finally look to the great spiritual and philosophical foundations of Europe and America, to Judaism, Christianity, democracy and capitalism, and be justifiably grateful for what we have accomplished as well as for what we have. The point is this: we have a lot to be thankful for, and yes, we can go to the movies, drive sports cars, and play volleyball in our bikinis, and be righteous, wisdom seeking, and compassionate. We can get off of our meditation cushions and then head for the beach. We can take a very connected walk in the woods during the day and then go out dancing that night. The ground is just as spiritually fertile in the West as in the East.

Furthermore, there is great promise here on our shores. This period we live in represents a great convergence, as well as a unique opportunity. The most affluent, technological, democratic, and yes, materialistic peoples of all time are increasingly looking away from the external toward their inner selves. It is only something positive that in the land of the free and the home of the party animal we are now looking seriously at the frontiers of consciousness, and to exercising compassion as well as our muscles. Sometimes the greatest benefit of a free society is the opportunity to find out that there is an even greater freedom than political freedom.

To people living several centuries from now, this extraordinary meeting of mindfulness, mysticism and material progress might rank ahead of computerization and space exploration. Why? Because it is one thing to have the great theories of Newton and Einstein, and the ability to create models for the cure of disease on a computer or to travel into the far reaches of space. It is quite another to use our theories and our tools with clarity of mind and a profound respect for all living things, in order to do good with our nearly godlike inventiveness. No one will ever forget what defensive brutes in armor and suits did with gunpowder and later on, atomic energy.

All the same, we do not need to repaint the great Western enlightenment with another coat. We have done well by it. But there is something perhaps even more important to consider. The present synergy of the science of yoga and meditation with our Western medicine and science, along with the mix of freedom, democracy and mindfuness is not only a positive cultural exchange, but likely *the essential change* which will allow us to achieve the next level of human civilization.

Through open-minded, scientific investigation, and mindful interaction with our local ecosystems, our planet, other peoples, and one another, we might actually be able to wake up together.

7

No Answers,
No One Way

THERE IS A QUALITY to Buddhist teachers and those who impart the unfettered wisdom of deep, clear seeing that a newcomer might label stingy, or even annoying. Why are they answering my question in such a strange and cryptic way, many have wondered. Why are they withholding the goods from us? Really now, what kind of strange mind game is this, where the answers are too often vague, confusing, or naught but a silent smile? Can't we get a straight answer here, please?

Why do so many wisdom teachers act like the Cheshire Cat? The reason is fairly straightforward. Only you can answer these essential questions for yourself. After all, most meaningful insights have to come from your own belly and your own experience. No one can think for you, no one can have insights for you, and no one but you can wake yourself up.

Precise answers to metaphysical questions can also be a dead end. There is a large difference between giving travel directions in a big city and giving directions for living and being. The mind is the player that runs interference between a wisdom teaching and our absorbing it fully, and the mind tends to take in metaphysical information and strain it for its own purposes, not unlike a carcass turned to edible ground round. The heart may prefer to merge with the butterfly's flight, while the mind tends to pull off its wings in order to study it. Questions are important, but there are times we just need to sit in the question (or be with the answer), rather than the old mental bite and swallow. There is rarely one right answer and there is surely no one way. Also, it might be preferable to allow wisdom to come through our nostrils and our skin rather than through the skull. Sometimes we are simply much better off not asking yet another question, just as we can be better off saying nothing. Besides, as my Jewish mother says, "Who listens, anyway?"

I love to analyze, philosophize and debate. I think I am especially wired for these mental gymnastics. It often felt like my very culture encouraged me to behave this way. Discussions can of course be fun, sometimes they are helpful, yet I am finding something interesting of late: I'm actually more relaxed, even happier, when I sit still than when I itemize.

So what's to talk about? Why all these books about ineffable experience? Why all these detailed articles, tapes and courses on Nothingness? *Why this*? Always a good question. My immediate answer is that we human beings communicate with each other because it is our nature to do so and because, more often than not, we care for one another. We share experiences, and given the opportunity most of us will try to lift others, friends and strangers alike, to a higher place. When we can, we pull other people up to the next plateau with us. This is what makes us human beings.

Part II is my sharing and my pulling. I call Part II my Zen Journal. In it I have included daily journal excerpts over a five year period, a period of my life that was full of growth, vitality and change. I have done this not only to share insights and to reveal what we sometimes call a pilgrim's progress, but to also show that there is rarely a straight path or bee line to waking up. I also want to offer some perspectives that might challenge common assumptions, and have us look at our human condition with fresh eyes.

I also share the fact that some of my own self-perpetuated foolishness and more engrained behaviors have not fully abated. But now my perspective is quite different. It is not about an awful little critic's list of fault's, or what's lacking.

Now I have realization sufficient to know that I am a part of all of This. Here I am, full-blown and complete, and there is nothing else I need to acquire to be whole. Our so-called self esteem issues tend to become tiny and even evaporate when there is no solid self to weigh, measure and find wanting. We are bigger than self. There is something much larger here that I am very much a part of. This is not a subtle distinction. It is the life-altering distinction of the Buddha's dharma. It is the common core teaching of all the great religions.

But it is easy to forget our true, beautiful transparency and great wholeness. We all forget easily and often. So it is essential to emphasize once again that nothing whatsoever can substitute for one's own practice, and meditation. At a given point we need do more than read and discuss, take classes and go to therapy. As the old Spanish saying goes, there is talking about bulls and there is being in the bullring.

Think of the mind as a container with a very slight crack in it. You can fill it with the golden nectar of wisdom but eventually it will seep out, to be quickly replaced by habitual thinking, rationalization, concepts, and all the constructs of our psyche, personal history and culture. Everyone who has ever spent time wrestling to quiet the mind—and to keep it quiet—will confirm that this is so. All the same, we can simply learn to sit with our mind chatter, and after a while, just like a persistant itch, it will eventually fade and disappear. Of course, the chatter, second guessing, comparisons, dissatisfactions, and fantasies will arise again, as surely as we will get hungry just hours after our last meal, and as surely as tomorrow will follow today. The heart beats, the muscles twitch, the mind chatters. This is why we— beginners and masters alike—continue to practice.

The Supreme Talent

There's something else going on here, something much larger and all-encompassing than the odd, funny nuances of the human brain and the various movie reels of our own individual psyches. Our brains, as large as they are, do have limits as well as innate tendencies. And while the human mind has many talents, one talent reigns supreme: it is brilliant at tying itself up in knots and getting lost in endless loops. Our minds are in fact our favorite diversionary toy. We tend to get lost, sometimes happily, in our fantasies, our theories, our plans, and our current ideas of what's so. Further, this brain of ours which can grasp, understand and appreciate the wisdom of the Buddha's teachings is *a large part of but not quite* the Big Mind that Wakes Up. More than our heads are involved here. One's entire being, whole and indivisible, is awakened, and it is awakened within the infinite cradle of an entire cosmos that is already enlightened just as it is.

After all, we are not separate from the stars, either in our material make-up or in the subtle essence of our energy. We know we are human beings and earthlings, but we are much more. So who, or what, is looking back at us from the bathroom mirror?

We are the Big Bang on two legs with a voice box. We are ever-changing energy, the living children of the whirling galaxies. We are a very real part of something mysterious, infinite and grand. So a large portion of the enlightenment experience is the most profound sense of intimacy. One is no longer separate from one's environment, or other people, or all the creatures, or all beings throughout space and time, or the entire universe, the seen and the unseen.

Asked if he was God, the Buddha said no. What are you then, the questioner asked? I am awake, he said. The Buddha awoke from his own isolated dreams to a living universe that was more wondrous, beneficent, and flawless than the greatest fairy tale. He awoke to a seamless existence, one without any real boundaries.

Suddenly nothing—or no one—was irrevocably disconnected.

But what are we to do with such incredible information? What do we experience, as the philospher Nietzche said, when after looking so long into the Void, the Void looks back at us? What happens when we go ever deeper within, down to the core, and wake up more fully? Is anything lost? And is anything actually *gained*?

To be profoundly awake is to replace the drama and the endless narrative of our lives (you know, the story that we're always the center of) with the transparency of Unadorned Being. It can taste equally salty and sweetly liberating. There is a feeling of release—as if you have gone from a statue made of stone to a tree bending in the breeze, or a block of ice turned to flowing water. Our sense of isolation tends to dissipate. We are finally able to shake our false identity, or see it for what it is.

Today, I look back and see that I often existed in an imaginary, self-constructed cocoon. At least that is how it felt. Ken saw the present through Ken's past. I mostly perceived the world through my own filter, and became lost in my own thicket. Yet I was also inclined to break free, to remove the bramble and thorns and step out to some new place I could not quite put my finger on.

Continual practice clears the thorny bramble. It is that one robust reminder that we-are-world, and we-are-cosmos, and that we were always whole. We arrive back at the place that we started from—our world, our animal nature, our senses—and indeed know it as if for the first time. This earth and this existence becomes more enchanting than anything that can be conjured by the human imagination simply because it is. We are lucid because It is lucid. It shines on, we shine with it. And once the doors of perception are cleansed, the door itself is unhinged from its jambs and disappears. If anything is Nirvana that is Nirvana: the death of the false self, the deathlessness of every moment, the land beyond birth and death.

That said, I want to let go of "enlightenment" and "Nirvana" and get back to our everyday lives. There is the pretty picture in the magazine and then there is the meal we actually cook from that recipe. There is Hollywood and then there is our hometown. There is the TV family and our own real family. There is how we think things should be and then there is the evening news. And once you wake up, there are still jobs and bills, head colds and heartache. Nor do the criminals. rapists, con artists, terrorists, maniacs and dictators suddenly disappear down some rabbit hole. Let us not be specious. The suffering of this world does not vanish in a puff of pretty pink smoke.

Here then are our very lives. Here is the jam packed living we must do. The folly and small victories. The hard and the soft. The love we gain and the people we lose.

The Only Constant

One of the great, enduring lessons the Buddha taught is the lesson of ceaseless coming and going. Everything that is alive or composite dies or transforms.

Everything we hold dear will one day be gone. Everything changes. Unending change and the transience of all things is a fundamental truth. Most of us fight this truth, this universal constant, few of us are comfortable with frequent or radical change, and for the most part we even deny our own transience. We feel more comfortable thinking we are solid, and not subject to certain universal laws. Alas, we can deny and deny unto our final breath, however . . .

In fact, this very book you are reading is about to transform. I am going from the initial narrative and overview to the realm of the more specific and personal.

The pages that follow are from my journals over a five year period (1997-2001), but what you will read are not the nitty-gritty details of my life. I have spared you my own drama. It is all personal, mind you, it could not be anything else, but it is more than my personal tale and a compilation of my own small triumphs and screw-ups. It is about process. It is also about seeing things differently. Twenty-plus years out of school, I learned. So if some passages read like I am teaching something, remember that this was first written to and for myself, and most spiritually-minded teachers are teaching not only what they have learned but what they still need to learn. As for this dharma student, I continue to learn, and now I walk into walls less frequently.

One unequivocal Zen homily states: a thousand mountain ranges separate the one who reflects from the one who is truly present. Or, a string of pearls of insight does not make for a necklace of enlightenment. Yet all I can do is share my own experience. The following selections are insights and rhetorical questions, not solutions or strategies. They are snapshots of my mind, but they are also the movement of one person's path, the unseen flower slowly unfolding.

By 1997, I had run my own advertising and marketing business for nearly 15 years with some success, become intimate with a number of fine people, and had traveled to a few more places around the globe. But more important than any of my modest achievements and attainments up to that point were these two events: my fiance was pregnant with our child and I had reignited my Zen practice with an earnestness and maturity that I had not engaged in previously. My life was in the middle of a profound "double transformation." One self-satisfying, forever clever rascal was about to break apart in order to become whole. Ken Taub was going to dig down, scatter dirt and plant seeds, only to grow into himself. I went deep, but I also went high. I went up to disturb the clouds so that fresh waters could reach the roots. The excerpts that follow are from that very fertile time.

Dig in. Read the pages that follow in order, or at random. Either way, I hope that what you read provides kindling for your own fire, and for your own practice.

Practice? What is it that we are actually *practicing*? Why do we need to dig deep and to grapple with our conditioning, our armor and our persona? Why do we need to do anything other than go about our lives? It is an excellent question.

My short answer is this: conscious living and clear seeing is the best work one can do and the best journey one can take because we are all here to do more than snack and talk about the weather. We are here in our magnificently designed, individual bodies for other reasons. Our bodies are our vehicle for liberation as well as for locomotion. Ultimately, there is no separation between our own lives and the Buddha's dharma. Both are precious, both are a gift. So perhaps we can practice in concert, and gently remind one another to use this greatest of gifts to awaken, to refresh heart and mind, and so doing, to answer all the Big Questions by one's self and for one's self.

So far as I know, there is no other way.

Part II

**Zen Journal
1997 - 2001**

I sit on the deck and look out,
taking my place
amongst the swift and vibrant tide.

IN THE BEGINNING OF 1997, I was still less than a year into my relationship with Lesa, the woman who would become my wife and the mother of our child. I was still months away from attending my first meditation retreat at Zen Mountain Monastery in upstate New York. While there were peeks past the mist, and peak moments, Ken was still operating almost exclusively in a realm of concept, detached judgment, and a structure built on history and personality. The man that this boy had become remained mired in a seemingly endless array of personal issues and subsequent entanglements. Here he was, another noisy personality hacking his way through the thicket. And hacking away, working only to survive in the jungle, how does self see Self?

Determination is one way. My desire to open up and to ease up had not waned; rather, it had grown. I wanted to break through, or break out, and so I kept an eye out for new openings. I looked inside. I saw what was happening—and what was not.

In the first few journal entries that follow I noted where I had been and where it was that I "needed to go." I was moving from the incidental to the intentional. I was going to dig digger and wake up, even if I had to somehow pry my own eyes open.

January 29, 1997

Ken has all these clever and occasionally illuminating thoughts about being and consciousness, and the boy attempts to thread the needle with ease and insight, and then an unnamed bird outside the window sings a few distinct notes and I shut my inner mouth for long enough to realize *I am that too.*

July 17, 1997

In meditation, when the past comes roaring forward, sometimes I become Mountain, where large and stone-solid, I sit still through all the pain, illness, tragedy, mistakes and mishaps. When current issues arise, I do not shun them, I become Fire, and here the flames happily consume everything, every small item, every so-called problem. Entering deeper meditation I become Air, a transparent membrane, a clear expression of molecules and energy, and an antidote to all melodrama and history. The world flows through me, I observe it and watch it enter and exit, and I let it go.

Other times I just sit and worry. And make shit up.

July 30, 1997

The moments I have been energy interpenetrating energy,
awake and nameless,
without a shadow,
an impartial observer,
keenly ahistoric,
simultaneously bygone and present,
a joyous warp in space . . .

and not the same old personality
protecting everything and projecting everywhere . . .

have been too few
and wholly missed.

August 11, 1997

*The summer, the season of year in which I was born, is often a
time of fun and ease for me. I could feel myself opening up. I could
even inject a sense of play into my own growth and inquiries.*

We have heard, "practice makes perfect." But in Zen
we can say, "our practice is never perfect," or equally, "the
instant we begin practice, it is perfect."

We sit, and the world aligns with itself.

When we stop talking to ourselves and look around,
we see. When we stop defending our positions and listen,
we can hear all of creation.

Just as the proper stance and holding of the bat is a hit
outside of time, and a well swung strike is air pregnant
with a home run, so as we silence our minds—just now —
and put aside our ever-changing personal agendas, we are
present, and we are awake, and we are complete *as we are*,
and we are sluggers, no less than Babe Ruth.

August 13, 1997

The manifestations of this nameless force, the mother
of all things, all phenomena, are humorous and wild.

Fire-breathing stars and dolphins, banana trees and
lemurs arise for the sake of arising, and to run free
through time, and to roar or laugh in their wild run.

Like a toddler breaking away from its mother, or a
teenager careening at high speeds down the highway,
here we are delighting in our temporary individuality,
and in our locomotion, and in our swim through space
and time.

We bark at the stars that birthed us and resist returning home, but of course we are always home, always a part of This and not apart.

We are a ball of gas and a giggle. And we are much more than we seem.

August 19, 1997

Passion. Zen practice is not a gray sky nor a desert. One must not subdue the passions (other than when it is practical to do so). One must practice with passion. If there is no passion to one's practice, one is a fish in very shallow water or a lone bird on a wire. Life is impassioned; the life force is dynamic and engaging and juicy. Why should's one's practice be passionless and arid? Life is passionate, practice can be no less. Breathe deep.

August 25, 1997

We are exhausted by living ahead of ourselves. In the moment there is no depletion. Even the Great Matter is decapitated.

August 28, 1997

How we attach to every big desire and little whim, even ones we have just made up . . .

A month ago or less I was happy with the cars we had. Now I'm attached to selling the Miata and getting the CRV, a vehicle I didn't even know existed back in July.

We make shit up, and then we desire it, and then rationalize our wants, and then we attach to our desires, identifying with them strongly enough to become them.

It's funny, a bit sad, strange, and very human. It's also quite interesting.

September 4, 1997

Be here now? As for living in the present, beavers and bees do it, my dog, some simple folk and infants do too. So-called primitive people mostly live in the present, as do porcupines and poplar trees. (*Are we in the present when we are dreaming?*)

Of course there is nothing wrong with good, rich recollection that becomes good, rich literature; recalling a happy moment; sexual fantasy; careening through space and time in one's mind; and simple daydreaming. The brain and our species need this.

So fierce awareness and existing *only* in the present isn't "perfection" or wholly desirable. We need our mental diversions. And let's not forget rapture, ecstacy, and a good shot of whiskey or wine every blue moon.

September 9, 1997

Let us assume we have acquired all the answers to the Big Questions . . .

We know in no uncertain terms there is a God, a divine Force, the Tao. Yes, there is a great Consciousness, a profound vibrating Presence to the cosmos, a Big Mind that is both of the physical universe and independent from it. We discover that there is indeed a love and a peace that passeth understanding. Life after death? Absolutely. We realize there is also death after life, deathlessness, endless regeneration, coming into being moment by moment, and no true separation between now and eternity. We have learned that there is some form of reincarnation. At the least, the results of our actions and our accumulated wisdom goes on. We know this body, this mind, this person, this personality dies, and we also know some energy goes forth after the body dies. We ask if there is a dynamic, intrinsic awareness—a form of underlying sentience or Buddha-mind—in all things, from cows and worms to mountains and rivers, planets and stars? We harmoniously agree that the answer is yes. We then ask, is God love? Our ultimate wisdom source says: "To be sure. Yet God is also mother's milk, Gandhi, Mao, the sun, the Milky Way, me, you, the breeze, the buzz of insects, the lion eating the antelope, the whole of humanity, a frog. Nothing is apart."

Okay, there you have it. We agree, here are all our "Big Answers." However . . .

1) How does this knowledge change our day-to-day behavior?

2) How does this information alter *this* moment?

3) How are you or the world changed?

4) What is this?

September 15. 1997

Individuality? We plants and animals are merely (and miraculously) the latest phase of collective effort. We are equally form and function; our architecture is our life. Specifically, we are the present collective organization of single celled organisms and simple cells gathered into more complex metazoan societies. We are not separate individuals for God's sake, we are aggregates.

Robert Pirsig and more than a few scientists are right: everything is an aggregate.[1]

September 29, 1997

When we grab the dog's leash and say, "Want to go

1. Robert Prisig, *Lila: An Inquiry Into Morals* (New York: Bantam, 1992), pp. 145-148.

outside?" he gets very excited. Once we wondered if while already outside, say in an open field, we took his leash to his face and asked again, "Want to go out?" if he would still be excited, thinking there is "more outside" to go to.

Is there in fact "more outside"? Is there a larger sphere in which this sphere resides? Is there a physical world-self, a place of Greater Nature and wider being? Are there hidden dimensions within this world that humans can not see?

We know there are different levels of awareness: bee, bat, cat, snake, dolphin, chimp, infant, teen, bushman, urban man, new mother, baseball player, yogi. Are these all facets of a larger diamond, or separate existences?

October 3, 1997

Lesa finds out she is pregnant. I am in a state of I-don't-know-what; an hour later we are on a large ferry crossing the Long Island Sound to Connecticut where I write the following . . .

The deepest gong
of the thickest bell.

The large boat moves upon
the moving world.
We read, then
look up.
No wisdom on the page,
only paper and ink;
nothing clever or preconceived.
Even the captain's chart, the sea map,
is on fire.
We cross the dark blue together.
An invisible ferryman steers

into the north wind,
grins.

The two of us sit
on the cushion,
yet the three of us
are smiling.

October 5, 1997

What are we? Who is it that is born?
Who is it that dies? With what do we
identify? We're sure that we know who we are
and what we are . . . aren't we?

"Who are you?" we are sometimes asked and we
moderns usually answer withour given names, our occupation, and our place of birth or current residence.

"I am John Ericson, a carpenter, from Oneonta, NY."

Rarely do we go deeper and say, "I am an earthling, a
mammal, a primate who analyzes nature, works with
symbols, tells stories, and wears costumes."

No one I know has answered the question using the
basic elements.

"I am a water being. All life began in the oceans, seas
and ponds, and I am more than two-thirds water, and I eat
plants that all need water and I need water, and I am primarily a sac of watery cells, blood, mucous, sweat, tears,
saliva, urine, phlegm, lymph, marrow, and a dozen other
fluids. I fish and I swim. I am water."

or . . .

"I am a fire being. My brain is powered by many bil-
lions of electrical charges. My multiple, never-ceasing

metabolic activities generate continual energy and heat, and I maintain an average internal temperature of of just under 100° Fahrenheit (while the worldwide climate averages perhaps about 60° year round). I am nourished by the sun and I produce my own heat. I am fire."

or . . .

"I am an earth being. I come from the earth and I eat the fruit of the earth. I have mass. I have bone, sinew, muscle, teeth, skin, nails, and fur like all other mammals and many other phyla. I play in earth's fields and sleep in its caves or houses made from trees. I am earth."

or . . .

"I am an air being. I stay alive only by breathing. I am a respiration machine, one that is part of a much larger respiration system. I am a creature of winds, currents and vital chi. I am composed of atoms, which are over 95% space, not matter. I am air."

So, John Ericson of Oneonta, who are you?

October 6, 1997

The rustle of something
call it wind dancing
in the
trees
or birds whistling to
their significant other's
hearts.

Call it affinity
or more wind
or stillness
if you like.

Green leaves

golden leaves
no leaves
a seasonless essence
this rustle of
something.

Here
this is our very living
these winds
these sounds.

October 26, 1997

When you have nowhere to run and in that canyon's tight, fearsome corner you can't breathe right, shit right, sleep right, nor even tie a simple knot, your eyes burn with ashen sadness but they barely glow, and your fingertips are nearly numb, and even that crazy autumn moon will not come to your rescue, for you are a muddy puddle that will not reflect . . .

Then it starts to rain. And you listen to the rain. And the consistent patter of the rain is comforting, and larger than one's own stupidity, and the judgment machine quiets down for a while, and you cradle your being in the drops of water falling from the sky.

November 8, 1997

Two mornings in a row, I sat and stewed. It has been my early morning silent rant. Popeye seated in zazen with hands folded, yet still swinging at the air. I don't become the world, I take on the world. Call it Brooklyn zazen. Or Ken's zazen.

This is it. I am a Brooklyn Buddha. I am a tough-monkey Buddha. I am a clever, verbose, passionate New York

Jew Buddha. I am Ken Taub Buddha. I will not become a mellow Buddha this time around. But guess what? That's pretty much okay.

These are the conditions that prevail.

November 13, 1997

Bliss?

If there were pure Bliss and only Bliss, if they were no hard edges and only Undifferentiated Being, no relative, no particulars, no birth and death, I think even God would be bored. In fact, it would suck.

There would be no earth, ocean, trees, or flowers. No melodic birds. All Bliss? Then no separation or isolation, but also no growth, no adventure, no laughter, no tears, no struggle and eventual transcendence. Naught but Nirvana? Then no discovery, no synthesis, no awe, no creativity. No Pyramids, no Paris, no Japanese gardens. No art, no Shakespeare, no Beethoven, no Beatles. All Self? All and only Radiant Glowing Perfection? Fine, but no romance, no lust, no purple mountains, no baseball, no surfing, no Cindy Crawford, no Cary Grant, no honey, no milk, no mothers, no babies, no babbling brooks, no snow, no polar bears, no white tail deer, no flutes, no guitars, no song.

No fun.

January 29, 1998

We moderns generally meditate to "improve ourselves." But it is not for self-esteem or the calming of fear and neurosis that one should sit in silence. Because while it is our eternal hope to someday subjugate the subliminal urges and make our sorry little interior selves somehow proud, this rarely happens; or to be more accurate, it happens only sporadically. And this may not be the wisest goal in the first place.

Why? Because we have been "moderns" for a very short time, and canny creatures struggling to survive for very much longer. We are animals and we are wary. It is often smart to be cautious and sometimes appropriate to be afraid. Our impulses to keep away large and snarling beasts who live in the deep woods, or marauders with fierce, painted faces go back a long way. In large part these impulses have kept the tribe together and kept the majority alive long enough to breed and get the rest of us to this point. We may, in fact, want to pay homage to the hairy night watchman, who scanning past the camp site squatting on his haunches, wide-eyed and wary, lives within all of us. Our ever protective great-great-grandparents reside within our genes and our synapses.

With this in mind, we should consider sitting in meditation not to "get better" or to "calm ourselves" but to be awake to *whatever* is happening; fearful, angry, protective or lusty thoughts very much included. The roots of our so-called neurosis may be our parents in small part, but for the most part it is our neurons which are to blame, wired as they are for great caution, for fight or flight, and to be on the lookout for saber toothed tigers, snakes, bears, and vicious hordes on horseback. Men and women may sit in silence, but nature always calls.

Surely, it is a worthwhile exercise to pull loving thoughts all the way up from our loins to our third eye; to visualize world peace; or to bravely inhale invisible poisons and exhale kindness. But it is no less worthwhile to sit with the beast and to be present to our dreadful imaginings and our deepest fears. For the longest time, this kind of thinking kept us alive.

Sitting then is for clear, full awareness. And to be completely, starkly aware one might want to sit with others beside the golden buddhas of the past or lovely female bodhisattvas of the future. We may also want to invite the slimy amphibian crawling out of the mud and the vulture with red carrion hanging from its sharp beak onto our meditation cushions.

February 11, 1998

If one sits long enough, one gets into the dirt. Lots of personal stuff comes up. Yet if one sits longer still, one gets under the roots.

Past personal history, past dreams and personality, mind reengages Mind. Go down far enough and the chattering, judgmental creature gets a glimpse of the Silent Source. Underneath our raging rivers lies a single still pond. Underneath the deepest roots lives the Dispassionate Observer, witness to all the drama and the pathos and the self-inflicted wounds.

Here the waters are perpetually fresh. Here there are no particulars and no waves. Here is our beginning and our end. Here we are.

March 10, 1998

There are endlessly arising feelings.

This person is bright, this one is slow . . . . I don't like the cold, I like it warm . . . I love her, he pisses me off.

But it all changes. And the person who had 100 feelings and opinions yesterday is not the same person today. Feelings are just reactions. They come and they go.

There are endlessly arising feelings. And the weather keeps changing too.

March 18, 1998

I wrote this letter to author, naturalist and Zen teacher, Peter Matthiesen, after meeting in dokusan, or private interview. A man worthy of respect and great admiration, as well as an earnest Zen practitioner, I clearly wanted to connect with him, share myself with him, and perhaps entertain him too.

Dear Peter:

Mu bursts forth, it can not contain itself . . .

At the Saganponack Zendo, Peter Muryo Matthiesen, Sensei, gives Ken Taub "MU!" after lunch, but before dinner.

First, and primarily, the distinct sound of Peter's MU rings around the sun and reverberates in mind's ear.

We may not see each other next month, and in response to the koan, I say that there—*right there*—is Buddha with dog on leash. But is Buddha walking the dog, or is the dog leading?

In a story by Kurt Vonnegut, he had otherworldly aliens observing life on earth, who duly reported back after some time that dogs ruled this planet. Dogs had apparently spent thousands of years training humans to feed, shelter, entertain and chauffeur them. Dogs were so clever, the alien scouts said, that they even got humans to find dates for them, hooking them up with the opposite sex. . . so while people actually thought the dogs were their pets, wiser observers deduced that the humans were actually the canines' slaves.

Does a dog have Buddha-nature? They might tell you, but they are too busy lounging, or getting coiffed and taking best of show. As for *this* MU:

Mu is the dog without the leash.

Mu is the dog without the Buddha.

Mu is the Buddha without the Buddha.

Mu is a spring walk in mid-March with a dog, two Buddhas and a newborn earth.

On the matter of shikantaza ("just sitting") and the white light experience, sans Ken Taub . . . During my first sesshin, I had a deep samadhi experience wherein body and mind not only dropped away but where breath and self interlocked with Big Mind. Everything was crystallized, yet soft and suspended, gently holographic. All was bathed in a golden aura—jewels and glowing embers of suchness suspended in one great awareness.

This "before-birth" experience, as you know too well, can not be shared verbally. All I know is that there was a sense of awe and bliss so profound that it remained with me during the next kinhin and stayed with me for another half hour after that. Of course, one immediately thinks that This Is It! This is the place I want to be, this is where meditation "leads to." Later, in dokusan, Shugen Sensei said in effect to simply enjoy the experience and keep sitting. Ah well . . .

So Ken's Zen is simple awareness and simple appreciation, with the occasional kensho or peak experience that comes along whenever the hell it decides to. I am not much interested in "acquiring" the Silence that existed one second before the Big Bang. I am simply too paltry to turn my back on 15 billion years of roaring thunder, whispering winds, babies' wails, and Beethoven. Besides, I kinda like it. So content to be one of the beasts who do zazen, I say dog mu to dogs, fool mu to fools, buddha mu to buddhas big and small, and appreciation mu to senseis, friends and loved ones.

I look forward to seeing you again. Gassho.

On March 23, Peter Matthiesen wrote back:

Dear Ken Taub

I enjoyed your clever letter and am in accord with (most of) it. Philosophically, its Dharma is sound enough, but experientially? I can't "take your word" for it. You must grasp it. And you must show me. So come again.

PM

April 24, 1998

This is a letter I wrote to one of my teachers, Bonnie Myotai Treace, Sensei, who is the leader of Fire Lotus Temple, then in New York City, and now in Brooklyn . . .

Dear Myotai Sensei:

You do not thank your mama for pushing you from womb to world, and you need not thank your sensei for pushing you from world to Self. It doesn't help to spit at heaven and it doesn't make no never mind to thank the inherent wisdom of a suchness that shines, but spit and say thank you we still do . . . . .

So I'm having a pleasant enough Cherry Blossom zazenkai in Manhattan . . . then the wheels come off the bike. And its being aware, in the fiber of your being, of everyone's labors which brought you this apple you're eating on the run, headed to that business appointment. Or having the simple effin' decency to at least thank the cow that gave its life before you bite into its broiled carcass. It's knowing that grizzled, rag-fitted old men on the gilded streets of Manhattan and small children—for God's sake, small children—are dying as we run off to the beach. It's having mindful patience—forget *compassion*—with your spacey co-worker or roughhewn boss. These are the tough ones.

Where is the edge of my practice? (the question she had asked me in private interview, "Where is the edge?"; which at first I did not understand, and which soon thereafter upset my apple cart, and my meditation). The edge of my practice is the edge of my awareness, and so at some moments it stretches brightly into the neighboring galaxy, while at other moments it is numb to my neighbor across the street, or to the one standing right next to me.

I lose my focus, I swim in self-indulgent fantasy or recrimination, and the whole world drowns . . . .

(I did not really expect a response but in early June I got one)

Dear Ken —

Its been good hearing from you about how the practice has been moving your life—a poem, an offering, an open heart. I hope your journey continues to unfold boundlessly.

In Gassho—
Myotai

May 9, 1998

If they already occupy the sky,
where do birds go to die?

Do they hide within the black roots
of a wise old tree?
Or do they dive down to the bottom
of some emerald sea?
Do they find a secret hole
in between the rainbow's bands?
Or do they go to sleep
within the oak tree's old hands?

Do they soar mightily
until they reach the sun?
Or do they simply fly
until their flying's done?
Do they glide northward
for all they're worth?
Or do they nestle silently
in the bosom of the earth?

May 13, 1998

We come into the world soft, round and sexless, and
we go out the same way. The ripe, well muscled, curvy,
highly desirable people we become is only a passing
fancy. It is as if we temporarily evolve into mating creatures; sharp of eye, firm of breast and so attractive to one
another. We get big enough and sexy enough for long
enough to perpetuate the species (and enhance the
drama), and then we go squishy again. If we live long
enough, we return full circle to the soft, gentle, unaggres-
sive state of simpler being, where sex is distant and repro-
duction is far from the matter at hand.

We largely go back to the way we began, our bodies
readying us to return to the Source. Old babies, we shrivel,
our skin hangs, we drool again. So doing, we get ready to
trade in our protoplasmic stuff for stardust and invisible
pulsations of a new, voiceless joy, which is also temporary.

May 24, 1998

*It is only weeks away from my son entering our world. I can feel
myself opening up, uniquely sensitive, aware.*

I lay under the spring oak and heard a black bird mutter something repetitive, soft and distinct.

100

I stood on the back deck and saw a crow dip its Sunday dinner of squirrel carcass into a small pedestal fountain.

I saw my son move within my beloved.

I noticed a single sprig of mint growing through the concrete patio.

All of this in one day.

June 1, 1998

The lightning comes and he jumps up on the bed and shivers. Then the thunder starts and the rains heavy up, and he can't wait to go out and play in the deluge. And so I let him. And so he does.

I was thinking of writing essays on "On Being" and "On Time" but now I'm drinking Chateau Montrose Saint-Estephe 1993 at 2:45 in the night-morning, and when you craftily mix a cabernet sauvignon with a merlot and a cabernet franc, Being and Time are no longer separate, nor are they assailable via essay. Besides, I like listening to what the lightning has written.

Now, we are powerful only insofar as we are a part of nature, which is powerful, and so we are. Like an elephant rampaging through the thicket, missing only trunk and tusk and tail, my son will come through the bush and into this world.

. . . And the thunder and the lightning rolled on, and it said Here I Am, and the old dog running in its rain said Here I Am, and my mate, day's away from birthing our son, laughed in her sleep and said Here I Am, and Abraham said to God Here I Am, and I will say to our son Here I Am, and the ants in the medicine cabinet and the elephants in the bush say Here I Am, and God says Here I Am, and we say, in response, Here I Am, and the grape, the grape grower and the grape drinker all say Here I Am, and each day and each moment says Here I Am.

So Here We Are together, separate and not-two, in the summer storm, as we are dying and being born, and sitting still and dancing, and writing and drinking this Grand Cru Classe Du Medoc in the rain and in the eternal present, and on and on and on until it stops, which apparently it never does.

June 19, 1998

Its all up in the air, and in pieces.
52 hours ago, my son came into the world.
And its a new world.

July 3, 1998

I just died and woke up again.
Bottle fed my son for the first time. Liquid peace.
Zazen don't have nothin' over rockin' and singin'
a 17-day old child to sleep.

July 13, 1998

This then is our enlightenment.
Golden coated cockers are our enlightenment.
The morning sun slipping through the sliding back door, and Cheerios.
Wise-ass radio deejays on the way to B2B advertising.
Reading Dogen while Natassia Kinski is on the tube.
Jogging through town for the sixteenth summer.
Twin lilac bushes.
Our neighbor, the Nissequogue River, rolling along.
Perfect July days.
Occasional orgasms.
Crying baby.

Dirty diapers.
Little sleep.

August 19, 1998

I am not a Buddhist, actually, nor do I wish to formally become one. I may bow to Buddha now and then, but I am bowing of course to Self, and to everything that breathes.

I very much like Jesus of Nazareth, and his teachings on grace, forgiveness, acceptance and God's love; or more specifically, God as Love. Yet I do not think it has helped matters much—and it may have been profoundly counterproductive—to have made this wise and courageous man into a supernatural figure. Part god, part superhero, part wishing well, part security blanket.

If you want to live a life of depth, make a difference in this world, and be a decent, caring human being, there are certain attributes and behaviors Jesus apparently had which are worth contemplating and emulating. Its really pretty easy to idolize and create myths, its much harder to do the hard work, and alter one's behavior.

The same goes for Siddhartha Gautauma, the Buddha. Many Buddhists believe that this man "reached Nirvana" or some suprahuman level of consciousness (indeed for many, "no reaching Nirvana, no Buddhism," and equally for Christians, "no Resurrection, no Christianity"). For a majority of Buddhists, this Indian prince of centuries past somehow transcended his own humanity. In other words, he was more than human.

While I appreciate their unparalleled accomplishments, I do not want to do either Buddha or Jesus a disservice by turning them into icons or plastic dashboard figures.

KEN TAUB

For me, Buddha amassed a great deal of courage and life-on-the-line commitment to achieve his great breakthrough. He saw into the foibles and shadow reality of human greed, ignorance, fear and defense, and then went past it for himself, actualizing the wild, free, timeless nature that he was and we are.

Like a bright 10-year old or an open minded scientist, he looked unflinchingly and deeply at the world, including human behavior, and saw things in a fresh, empirical, unusually receptive way. Seeing the world completely free of preconception and superstition is no small feat. God knows, this is hard enough.

Buddha, in short, woke up. And he woke up not because he was a god or a magical being to begin with, but because he learned to think anew. The clear-headed former prince saw the world and himself as one, and he saw this self-world not through the fearful, reactive, hissing, lizard-monkey brain, or through the only partially conscious dreams and symbols brain, but with his whole brain, and his whole belly, and his whole being, which is, first and last, the brain of the world and the brain of all nature.

Worship Jesus and Buddha if you will, but do so at your "peril." Because you can idolize Babe Ruth or Tiger Woods, or you can go out and hit some balls. You can idolize Jefferson, Emerson or King, or you can educate yourself and participate in the larger arena. Practice is not worship, waking up is not a new belief. If you observe your behavior, observe your observations, remain steadfast, meditate, dig down deep, and then look around once more, and *see*, and do this in the context of simple decency and simple awareness, you too can be a superhero. Or at least a human being so fully human that you occassionally resemble one.

September 26, 1998

This was a powerful insight-experience I had, full-bodied and whole, which occurred in a just few moments while driving. I tried mightily, but it loses a lot (if not just about everything essential) once it is written down. Therefore the primacy of first-hand experience. Therefore zazen.

Take the grid off New Jersey, eradicate the man-made map, forget the tolls and the state legislature, and there is what is there. There is no *real* New Jersey (yes, even with the tolls, taxes and the state legislature).

And there is no real anything overlaying this moment and this place, and that person or that thing, and that fleeting physical sensation. But we make our grids, our maps, our names, our analyses, our observations, our reductionism, our concepts and our reactions into The Reality we abide in. These thoughts, opinions, generalizations, ideas and preconceived notions we create ***have become our lives*** (whew . . . big exhale . . . stay still for a minute).

Rarely but rarely do we see what is in front of us unhindered, whole, without judgment, with all of our senses and all our attention, stripped bare and receptive. And so we live in our heads, we rarely live in the world.

And so, and so, and so . . . to strip away, and to strip away again, and then once more, and to see clearly and to pinch ourselves . . . then we might breathe a full, unencumbered breath. To be a part of the always mobile community and not a judge seated on high is to be alive, and free, and finally, sane.

September 27, 1998

Consciousness, present from the first moment of conception, now blooms in my three month old son without hesitation or apology . . .

Yielding to nothing but the dictates of its own happy hunger; this mouth of earth, this godly eye, this breath of sunlight and a farther universe . . .

It is here again, this spectacular expression of something grand, something both subtle and omnipresent, this life of bright eyes and appetites, this lovely physicality, this endless mind-begetting-mind . . .

This babe on the bed.

November 6, 1998

We hear it, we're not deaf.
The gathering wind, the long chimes
ringing across the yard.
Then we lean, cup our ears and listen
all the more carefully:
the plaintive wail three miles south . . .
the Honduran cigar tapped, the tight ash
gliding to the ground . . .
the strong chill in the evening air,
the cold so cold it whispers.

When the gliding crows caw in harmony,
the sun goes down early.
Perfect sounds generate magical results.
Like late autumn light,
which when wrapping half naked boughs,
sings like the white recoil of a whip.
November sunlight itself sings;
penetrating our backs,
and pausing briefly,
it actually crystallizes into a song
some druid might have sung once,
a long, long time ago.

We do not pretend to make sense
of this vast, vibrating prism . . .

But we hear it,
we're not deaf.
We just don't know what to do
with such beautiful noise.

February 5, 1999

What is convenient for the brain is not necessarily reality. It may be efficient or even innate to perceive something this way or that, but it doesn't "make it so." The
only thing that is *So* is endless motion, ceaseless change
and a boundless, borderless, dynamic, interrelated whole.
It moves, for God's sake.

We see what we can see, we hear what we can hear,
we taste what we can taste, and even with our amazing
instruments, we only see and hear and taste so much.

We get this and not that. We catch this event and miss
the smaller one underneath, or the larger event which this
thing happens to be just one piece of. We capture one
thing or one experience and we treat it as a snapshot and
we put a caption underneath it. Then we walk away,
thinking that we have understood, that we have grasped
the larger dynamic, when all we have is a fossilized bone
or two in our desk drawer.

The human brain is just one very small piece. And the
firing of neurons is quite interesting, but it is just the firing
of neurons.

March 17, 1999

I am thinking of the truth of wildness . . .
While Zen adherents incorporate a series of refined

actions in their practice—sitting perfectly still for an hour or more, bowing, mindful walking, ceremonial meals and tea ceremonies—this is merely artifice and contrivance; albeit exacting, helpful contrivance. For the heart of practice is the beating heart of life, which is to say nature, innate freedom, ceaseless change, randomness. In short, wildness.

If civilization is in large part meant to keep us civil, and to keep out wolves and bears and our own animal nature, then the many refineries of Zen—Japanese Zen especially—can be seen as the pinnacle of civilized behavior. We are told to practice ceremonially, in constraints of sorts, with the ultimate goal of being finally free and unfettered. The precise manners and skillful means of Zen Buddhism are designed, oddly enough, to create a new kind of wild man or wild woman. We are wearing robes and sitting still to realize we are naked and unrestrained.

Since nature is boundless and generally unpredictable on the larger level; since it is juicy, messy, bloody and brimming with death at all times; and since we are an integral part of this terrible beauty, this joyous mess, then it does seem strange, doesn't it, to reign ourselves in so in order to see that we are naturally unbridled?

But what we are doing, I guess, is finding a quieter, sometimes peaceful and somewhat more "civilized" way of allowing one wild system (me) to support and interact more easily with another wild system (you), so that we can all live more harmoniously with the larger wild system (our environment and the rest of Life).

So? Zen is only a garment, not new skin. It is a stepladder, and not the end point we are reaching for. Our own skin is our true robe. Our saliva, our finest tea.

March 30, 1999

Desire flares like a hot wind. And the hot wind takes itself mighty seriously at first, before it recedes into a thin chuckle. Or resentment. Or boredom. Or the next thing. Or nothing.

We are hungry for this person or that thing or that goal, and more of all of it, until the hunger dissipates, fading to a kind of transparency, allowing us to finally see through the thing, back to ourselves.

It can be exciting, sure. It can feel good, don't we know it. And it surely makes for a great deal of drama, this desire element. It can also be a very big waste of time in a very short life.

May 21, 1999

Who is it that writes this?
Who is it that reads this?

We say that our mouths, our dicks and our stomachs have "a mind of their own." In actuality, what is primary is that our minds have a mind of their own. Rarely, and not for long, do we identify with our stomachs or our genitalia, but we do identify with our thoughts, such that what our brain thinks we think we are.

So what is there? Where is one located? Knock, Knock. Who is it? We keep on looking and looking and finally we find no one home. We know we exist, but where? In this skin and only within this skin?

Where are we?

May 31, 1999

Is there real growth in our practice? Do we transform? Do we become somehow profoundly different? Does Jane Smith or

James Jones move out so Buddha can move in?

We think, "Oh yes, twenty years on the mat and I'll achieve selflessness." Like we can actually transform and go from an ego-container to an empty glass, from somebody to Nobody.

Here is what I have found to be so . . . that we inhale and exhale, and we are busier and quieter, and sometimes we are the cooking, or raking, or walking, or playing the piano. And sometimes we are our troubles, real or imagined.

To put it another way, self and selflessness come and go like the breath, all the time, from birth to death, thousands of times a day, in and out, no less than daydreaming and presence, muddled thought and clarity, worry and activity.

Self and no-self are always present like light and shadow. or the image followed by the black square that make up the movie reel we see. In and out, appearance and disappearance, stepping in shit and stepping into open space, ego and no one, all the time, every day, all of us.

That is what I have found to be so.

July 5, 1999

Before the birth of a two-legged Buddha
(and before a certain scribe wrote,
"Let there be light!")
there was the round and hardy trilobyte.
Now it swam in the ocean
before "ocean" was a word,
and it flew in the water
before dinosaur became bird.
It was a part of the whole,
and the whole, in part,

and it loved to locomote
with all its primordial little heart.
It swam as it swam and it was as it was,
and Wisdom rolled in the waters with no below,
no above.
Distinctions arrived
along with the first grunt,
just as politics were born
along with the first hunt.
But once nothing was lost
and nothing was gained
by being wildly alive
with barely a brain.
And once you could speak your mind
(in the very beginning)
by saying nothing,
and just swimming.

August 19, 1999

I finally noticed this neatly concealed box hidden under my bed. On it was a label which read "What Really
Matters." I was nearly dizzy, and not for the life of me
could I figure out how I missed the box for all this time.
Anyhow, when I opened the box there was another box
that once opened had a little slip in it that read, "Not Enlightenment." Immediately, I noticed a second, smaller
box, which I grabbed and opened. It read, "Not Wisdom"
Sure enough, there was yet a third box that contained
these words, "Not friendships. Not influence. Not efforts.
Not accomplishment." I guess I was a little surprised or
maybe an iota perplexed, and about to walk away scratch-
ing my head when I noticed a very small box with a ribbon delicately wrapped around it. I carefully removed the

ribbon and looked inside the smallest box.

It read, "Kindness matters."

August 22, 1999

So how does one know how one is doing? You can always ask your guru or your sensei. Of course, they don't give grades. Besides, if you have to ask another to authenticate your own experience or deeply felt insight, well, then . . .

Okay then, how do you "score " your practice?

Its fairly easy. There's more: acceptance, empathy, patience, attentiveness to people, attention to the task at hand, freedom from want and fear, and comfort in one's own skin.

There's less: judgment, anger, fear of death, unquenchable desire, isolation, comparison, confusion, and getting in one's own way.

Eventually, you have no concern about scoring yourself in any way, shape or form. At that point, you've "passed."

September 20, 1999

We don't know the name for the wind, or where it ends and where we begin, or why the sky is so effortlessly blue, or at what point we stopped being star field or starfish, if ever.

There are so very many names for the magic acts of creation that we get lost swimming in our vast vocabularies, and we forget that the puppet stage is essentially an empty box, space in other words, and that everything comes from an unimaginably fertile nothingness, and that every blessed thing is more nothing than something, more space than substance.

As children we delighted in each sudden appearance

of this thing or that character as it popped up in the puppet box. We knew it was magic, and new, and as fleeting as it was sudden. Somehow, we get older and forget.

October 5, 1999 Santa Fe, New Mexico

In the 30 years since I have been to the Tassajara Zen Center, what has changed? Everything has changed, even as I have managed to retain that boy within me, both to my vitality and detriment.

Now I am back out West, with a boy of my own, seated smack in the middle of life, in the affluence and in dhukka, the perceived lack, in the joy and the suffering, in the night and the deeper night, and in the center of the heart, which is close to the moon and the stars.

I am uncommonly common. I am surely common in that I am living my separate life, along with everyone else. We do not live as if we are a part of something larger and mysterious, we live as if we are indeed separate, and apart. We generally live with our eyes shut, and when they are open we manage to avert our gaze from all the glory.

I look in the mirror and I can still see that boy who, wide eyed and excited, drove up the winding dirt road to Tassajara. There is the fresh beginner's mind and there is the little buffoon, still managing to work together.

November 29, 1999

(after accidentally running over a squirrel on the way to work)

You start off the day with murder and you end it with mercy, and however unintentional both were, you are at once the killer and the forgiven, and it is at this improbable intersection of savagery and salvation that truest Mystery is born.

For 200 centuries the embodiment of this Mystery has most often been someone named Jesus. And while this bright and anguished man may have been anybody, or may have been a gift from God, there is little doubt that he is a lamb, and a vessel of hope, devotion and a larger possibility, as well as the supreme vessel of sacrifice.

Now aside from being a titanic celebrity of the Spirit, this man's image is also alluring and comforting. For me, he has always been quite interesting. So while some dismiss the whole story as legend, and while others exalt him onto the very Highest, I remain endlessly curious and forever compelled by this personification of grace, courage, forgiveness, acceptance, and extraordinary decency.

He is a nice figure to gaze upon and a nicer presence to have around. When one is about to be consumed, when a loved one is ill, or even after one runs over a smaller creature, Grace and Forgiveness with a human face is most reassuring.

And while I do not worship, I do offer this beautiful man acknowledgment and respect, and would not be ashamed to kneel at his feet.

December 21, 1999

It is getting wintry out, and the Oh-Ohs are coming. We lose our kingdom for want of a moment's quiet, and we conjure up dread because someone decides to flip a calendar page.

Elmer Fudd says, "Oh, da hor-wah," and Bugs Bunny, Brooklyn born Zen Master, hushes him by kissing him on the mouth.

And sometimes we shudder, and sometimes we laugh, and often we sigh.

But we might remember this: "That a kiss is just a kiss, a sigh is just a sigh. The fundamental things apply as . . . "

January 9, 2000

You start by having compassion for Kenny. That boy you thought you knew so well. You start with him, and you move on from there. Who are you going to take good care of until you can cradle yourself?

Next you come home. One roosts one's compassion there. Its critical. It's where the heart is. Then your compassion can hit the road.

Eventually you gain compassion for the moments. All of them. They are mayflies and fading light. They're all you've got. And they're dying.

Running across the field with babe and old dog, wind in the trees; walking slow and wordless in kinhin with Nick and David; sharing soup in the winter house, quiet and warm; Jake's precious laughter; Peter's silly phone messages; the cold that hits you when you first exit the front door; the bare branches against the open sky.

February 15, 2000

Early morning.
These pajamas have no pockets.
Squirrels, already up for hours, chatter energetically.
Someone says: paring down facilitates sanity,
and wholeness.
Right now we own nothing, and we are nearly
ecstatic.
There is that crumb on the floor and that one
ray of sunlight
coming into the kitchen.
Now we are rich.

The house is bone quiet.
Suddenly the dense gray skies open up completely.
The explosion of water is the patter of pleasure.
Rain dances with rain.
He drinks from the wooden ladle.
He leans into what he drinks, and leaves some for
itself.

Water goes to water.
Throat gulps in small rhythms of gratefulness.
Toes wiggle on the soggy ground.
Mountains shimmer.
Wet tongues wag.
They say: circulate.

The rivers bow to the clouds.

February 21, 2000

I saw a powerful photo that had this caption: "The abbess of Gioji Temple in her studio. During her youthful days she was a famous geisha. Kyoto. 1963." Once she provided comfort and pleasure for others, years later she offered comfort and presence for others. And for herself.

We struggle and we fight. We get hurt, we hurt others. We defend, we get angry.

We can turn away or push people away. We can be mean and petty and small. We are quick to react, and most of our reactions are thoughtless and selfish, and based on fear or conditioning. We commit sins. Little ones. Grave ones. We sell our bodies and our souls for money, pleasure and power.

But rarely do we freeze. And sometimes all it takes is the smallest warm breeze.

The opportunity to absolve ourselves, trust ourselves and even transform ourselves is great and constant. Our genial humanity and the natural expression of simple decency is generously available at all times. We can reclaim our hearts whenever we wish, on any day, at every one-hundreth of a second.

Grace is as real as gravity.

March 4, 2000

It is not my intention to be serene, celibate and cosmic. It is my intention to be centered, sensual and earthy.

For me, this Buddha-nature is not about merging with the Absolute. It is not about adopting an empty sack. That is an allegory, not to mention unrealistic.

A clear and positive mind is a clear and positive mind. We do not live our day-to-day lives measured by ideals. We do not go up to a mark on the wall each morning that is drawn at 6'2" when are fully grown adults and but 5'10". Walking purposefully is still walking, running frantically is still running.

We have a lot to do; we have our lives to live.

And so we make yet another choice. We can attempt to merge with Nothingness, or we can passionately accept . . . . *being alive.*

Who will raise their hand when asked if the Great Void beats the Grand Parade?

Is not the real Middle Way living this life most fully?

March 13, 2000

Silence. And the wisdom thereof.

You take the label off the avocado, and there it is, the whole black-green, nubby-smooth, Vitamin E-rich alligator pear of it. With or without the label, the avocado is still the tangy fruit of the American tropics, the fatty, tear-shaped breast of southern California, the edible testicle of Texas.

I slowly turn this fruit I am about to eat in my fingers and wonder how green I will be in a half hour. I do not know. I do know that, upon close inspection, the avocado is quite beautiful. And the three speckled bananas, those smiling golden herbs from Lotus Land which are now sitting in our hanging copper kitchen basket, could not agree more. Only they say nothing after they smile and nod. They simply sun themselves in the scaled-down flood of indoor light, the essence of still-life, silent and knowing.

March 14, 2000

There is a path out of the thicket.

And I think that one night I will have the will and the courage to stay up all night seated on my meditation cushion and answer all the questions and get all the right directions when I employ the right determination, as if my life depended on it.

And then I think that all my answers, or the one big answer, will just bring me back into the thicket.

And then I say stop thinking.

And now I know what they meant when they said, "Shh. Just have a cup of tea."

April 1, 2000 In Delray, Florida with the old Jews

How do you get from here to there? Ask a Catholic and they will answer, "Pray, and you will find your way." The Protestant says, "Take the most direct route, and go with God." The Muslim says, "Only Allah knows." The Hindu proclaims, "There are many paths to the same place. The Buddhist answers your question with a question, "Why bother going *there*?"

And the Jew says, "I can tell you, but you probably wouldn't want to know."

They are too comical, these people. My people. Pushed about, endlessly exiled, blamed for everything but the weather and so long suffering, they became wily, and ironical. Then again, these former desert people, the ones who "crossed over," are more than simply your witty, consummate survivors. They represent God as Jokester; God as spinner of labyrinthian plots and cigar-chomping producer of nail-biting cliffhangers; and above all, God as Vaudevillian. One of the things we were Chosen for was to get pushed, shoved and persecuted throughout much of history, and then kibbitz about all the heartache and heartburn. Perhaps that's why its sometimes easier to find God in the Catskills than in temple.

Buddha was right of course. Life is full of suffering. But before the suffering starts—and especially after it— comes the great guffaw. The place where ignoble suffering merges with crowning achievement is also the place where we let go a little cosmic giggle, and hear the thunderous Divine Laugh.

Underneath the darkness is often dark humor. Behind the veil of tears, and hidden directly beneath all the small nicks and greater afflictions is this: an infinite wry smile, not lacking in kindness.

April 21, 2000

I get up early in the morning mist and watch Yukon Jack's golden fur gently heave. It reminds me first of the ocean's rhythmic waves, and then what arose from the mothering ocean. It is all so quiet, so very, very quiet.

And then, one by one, orchestra member after member, the wave crashing sounds of morning: thrushes, jays, lonely train horns, car doors, engines, youthful laughter down at the corner, the lifting of the fog. All the sounds come together until they are inaudible. Many things become One Thing.

Then it is quiet again. Breath melts into capillary and flesh. Tides go out. As for this observer, the early riser in the mist, he thinks he can nearly see the silent net, and the thread that winds its way across and through this percussing world. Boom, stitch, boom, stitch. And on and on, until there is no thread and until there are no separate beats. And suddenly there is only one sound. And no sound. And no there. And no observer. And no capillaries. And no ink left in this pen. Right now and forever.

Many things become One Thing. One Thing, many. Mist turns to Tchaikovsky. John Philip Sousa turns to sod. The dog breathes gently, even as he dreams.

June 23, 2000

Early this morning, I effectively began my day with the disembowelment of a Gypsy Moth caterpillar.

It was murder one, make no mistake about it.

Now these prolific critters flagrantly munch away at leafy trees (my trees!), so I take their being from their bodies when they get too plentiful (and have the temerity to cross my way). It seems that I place greater value on the fifteen large trees surrounding my home than I do on their propagation.

Later on that same day I came upon another Gypsy Moth caterpillar, only he was draped over an abstract three-stone Buddha I had recently created and placed next to my driveway. I watched him for a minute, and then I let him be.

I was done with work and had come outside to stretch before my late afternoon jog. Apparently, I was a more expansive being at 5:15 p.m. than I was earlier in the day. So seeing a little caterpillar seated on a stone representation of the Enlightened One, I instantly absolved him. I figured he was seeking sanctuary like Quasimoto in the cathedral. I honored his wish not to be squished. The end.

The moral of the story? We are breathing and thinking all the time, and mostly we breathe good air and think that we are decent people. But compassion, for nearly every single one of us, is largely arbitrary. We are compassionate when it suits us. Plain and simple.

Once we start with that simple and unabashedly naked truth, we can be honest enough with ourselves to know that exhibiting pure, unceasing compassion is harder than running 100 miles non-stop. When it comes to unconditional compassion, it serves no one's purpose to be idealistic and softly out of focus. We are monkeys who have been throwing stones and spears for 100,000 generations. We are the upright creatures who love to hoot and holler and point our crooked fingers. That said, we are good to each other more often than not, and that may be enough.

So go ahead, tell me about compassion. How many people have to come and go on this earth before we produce a precious freak like Mother Teresa?

Then again, is there any entity or any being in this universe with boundless, unconditional and flawless compassion, and filled with naught but compassion?

Are you sure?

July 9, 2000

A quiet eats the day.
The windmill, covered in a shroud of ivy, aches
quietly.
The air is still, the blades do not turn.
In the distance there is movement.
Now the great gray clouds are gathering.
A delicate oval rock quivers like a chick-laden egg.
Blades of grass begin to dance.
The highest leaves in the oldest trees sashay
in anticipation.
There is a fluttering exodus.
Local birds take off to unseen hiding places.
The ground politely rumbles.
I sit on the deck and look out,
taking my place amongst the swift and vibrant tide.
The sky above is densely serious.
The very air has become perilous.
Pebbles shake themselves loose from the soil
to glance up at the sky.
Particular atoms begin to rotate in reverse.
Tree limbs start to steeply sway.
It trembles.
Then gray and solemn, everything begins to interlace,
not unlike the fingers of many meditating hands.

Then the premium silence.
Then flash.
Boom.
Crack.
Here it comes.
It is furious and full of beauty.
It is our essential cord and our cutting knife.

The wind hurtles forth, it binds and
it slices.
All the loose pieces are shorn.
Now we are being born,
another wet being
in a fiercely joyous windstorm.

August 14, 2000

Unborn and unceasing . . .

More than winter or August breezes, one must have
the mind of all the suns and the planets, the volcanoes and
the rain, the first flowers, and the one who ushered the
very first grunt of astonishment. One must have the mind
of the ones who sat around the first campfires, and of
those who dwelled in the desert 7,000 years ago, and of
our grandparents. Then, and in an unrecognizable instant,
one must have the mind that existed one millionth of a
second before the Big Bang.

One does.

The paramecium, the sand crab, the cheetah, the bear,
the baboon. All peoples. Everywhere. The parade marches
within us, with us, past us. All of it, every lovely precious
tiny grand breathing spinning bit of it goes forth. Oh the
joy of seamless teamwork. Oh the tranquil hush of being
indivisible.

The spider's web covers my head.

August 19, 2000

We gather in the church basement room to support
one another's frail humanity.

We are broken, vulnerable, wildly imperfect, and of
course, frightened. But one by one we stand up and give
voice to our wrongdoings, and confess the wars we have

fought in and the wars we have initiated. After a few brave souls speak, it is my turn. I stand up and clear my throat.

"Hi, my name is Ken and I'm addicted to commentary. " The group responds in unison, "Hi Ken." I continue. "I'm also addicted to judgment, sarcasm, unsolicited opinions, cynicism, contrariness, cutting remarks, debate, nay-saying, gossip, unconstructive criticism, harranging, teasing, rambling, complaining, blaming, brief hostile remarks, name-calling, negativity, flowery BS, callous disregard, thoughtless statements, verbosity, verbal abuse, and everyday bitchin' and moanin'."

I exhale so loudly I hear it myself. I can not tell if I am pale or slightly red-faced. The leader of the support group says, "Very good, Ken. Anything else?"

I shake my head. "No, not today. That's it for today."

September 10, 2000

I have some knowledge about a few things but I don't know much about flowers, and for this I'm grateful. I do not know the names of too many flowers, bushes or trees; I'm no botanist. So when I come upon a field of many flowers, I am delighted. My lack of knowledge frees me. For all I see is a dazzle of color, the vibrant glee swaying above the soil, earth's shimmering bounty.

I am aware that some flowers and plants provide food for bees, occasional fruits for mammals, and certain tonics for pain or sleeplessness. But most flowering plants do not feed or medicate, they are just there bending in the breeze and being in their beauty. Flowers primarily exist for their flowering.

December 12, 2000

Our pervasive sense of self entangles us, even near the end.

In the past two weeks, my partner's 92-year old father died, our friends' 52-year old friend collapsed suddenly, and younger friends' 6-month old fetus stopped moving.

Where did they all go? To what new sunlight does the coma or the occupied uterus lead? How different are our life forms from the unceasing essence that brews in the the invisible vat of forever-becoming? Are we like the unique forms separated from the warm waxy mass within a lava lamp, shot off into space only to soon return to the larger mother glob? No? So it's a water planet. But then why do drops of spray temporarily separated from the big water-fall need to put on name tags?

How strange is it that the face we have after we are ex-pelled from the womb rarely recognizes the face we had before? And why is it that the blood in our veins and the marrow in our bones understand essence and origin, while the glowing cells in our brain do not?

December 17, 2000

I carried the aged pup down the back steps and into the windstorm, the sky dark, the earth turbulent, myself naked from the waist down, he pissing into the wind while in my arms, his heart failing, my mind a spectacular mix of all the elements and the keen instinct to protect, to survive at all costs.

We held on. The storm subsided. The newest morn-ing has come, quiet and benign. His heart is still beating, he is still with us. And I am here, writing this.

February 6, 2001

Not chasing. Not feeling chased.
Not wanting for much. Attached to less.
Not concerned about my status.
After all, who is it that cares?

February 27, 2001

Grand Master Kong of Yonkers, New York was cornered by one of his students one day. The student was earnest, and wanted to delve deep. "What can you tell me about going through time, past the Big Bang, and understanding all of it, and I mean all of it?"

The Master said, "A bowl of Cheerios."

We can sit with this one for a long time. Or say nothing, and chop wood. Because when it comes down to this bowl of cereal, here we are. It is not about the cereal floating in milk, or about the blue ceramic bowl, or the marketing of the cereal, or eating it, or not eating it. Its not even about little circular oats as nutrition. Its just about the Cheerios. That's it. There they are. And here we are.

A robot can pose this question, and those who will listen will get it. There's nothing not to get. Cheerios are Cheerios. The case is closed, so opening it up will only get you in a thicket of trouble. Looking beyond the Cheerios will not get you anything. The man from Yonkers stated something that goes beyond the Big Bang, and beyond the timeless minds that speak about the great event.

The whole thing brought us this bowl of Cheerios, and a bowl of Cheerios is the whole thing. We like this cereal, it is a lot like us. (with apologies to Eihei Dogen)

March 5, 2001 , Punta Cana, The Dominican Republic

When you're on vacation, and the seas are emerald

and the weather is perfect, and the beach is ringed with palms, and a significant percentage of the women are topless, and there is capable childcare, and the biggest decision of the day is archery or volleyball, the trap is set and fully secured.

For when there is nothing external to bother, stress, harass, or pull one there is only one place left to look: one's own mind. Here, in paradise, the little bugger still chatters away. It judges, defends its positions, pigeonholes, and tells the rest of you that, yes, you *still* suck, despite the tropical breezes. The fiend is relentless. It hardly ever stops to take a breather. It bogs us down. Its a heavy weight. It builds every conceivable wall and then slams its own nose into it. Having a mind should qualify all of us for disability insurance.

There is a four-part blue world and a dome, and no dome, and Big Mind and no-mind, and a recirculation of every wave and particle. Things are born only to become other things. Its a beautiful blue world, beautiful and awesome and fierce.

And smack in the center of the flowing blue suchness we have created a shipwreck. It sticks up out of the water like a lone, broken, rusty umbrella on a virgin stretch of beach.

We do this, stick something foul or flat unnecessary in the middle of the scenic picture. We litter Big Mind, we litter the world. The good news is that we put it there, so we are the ones who can remove it.

March 25, 2001
What's real?

The sun is now streaming through man-made glass over my right shoulder onto the facing page. Is this sun "less than" the sun we find outside, unframed and suspended in the beginningless sky? Is it less bright? Less warm? Less real?

There is the spider here on the sidewalk, the spider outside the window, and the picture of the spider in the book. There is the avian cacophony of morning, and there is Led Zeppelin on the car radio.

Phenomena are phenomena. The thing before you is it.

April 10, 2001

Yukon Jack dies at 13 years, 9 months

The carpet still has your moisture upon it. Remnants of your living fluids are still here. And the dirt with which we covered you, late this afternoon, is still under my fingernails.

Goodbye, my sweet friend. You were a delight and a blessing. I often thought it was we who took care of you; quite often, it was you who watched over us.

We love you, Yukon. Very much.

April 14, 2001

He died in between Passover and Easter. He entered stage left, a little blond fellow from Iowa. He exited a little less blond, coughing like an old Jew making his cranky presence felt in a geriatric facility. In the nearly fourteen years we were fortunate to share together he was our link to the real world —the world of sights and smells, spontaneous reactions, running through parks and fields, swimming in the ocean, rock climbing, This canine surely did not miss TV, video, computer games, or the damn Internet. He was not below these things, he was way beyond them. He felt ever so much of the natural world, and he smelled nearly all of it, He was our nature boy, never cast from Eden.

Now he's a part of the whole circle, and a free element, flying in the great whirl. He is not here, and he is still with us. He is free, yet he lives on.

Happy Passover. Happy Easter.

April 23, 2001

After sesshin at Zen Mountain Monastery

Paraphrasing what John Daido Loori, abbot and founder of the Mountains and Rivers Order, said at the end of sesshin . . .

How you ring the bell,
is how you sit upon the cushion,
is how you cook a meal,
is how you drive your car,
is how you clean your house,
is how you do your work,
is how you raise your child,
is how you live your life.

May 12, 2001

How far do the sun's rays travel
to warm my bones in May?
How incandescent is a second?
This morning I saw three black birds flying in
formation.
They cut across my sight, before making an arc to
the southwest.

Tell me, where did they go?
Tell me this as well:

How old is that neighboring star that hits our
eyes at night?
What faraway suns choose to speak to us with light?
And did you happen to catch what they said?

I have been in this house almost 20 years.
My son is almost 3 now.
He asks me what time it is.
I tell him I don't know.

Now he plays in the ancient backyard, running naked
with the garden hose and watering the babies,
as he calls the new growth and the infant grass.
Then he laughs as he sprays the world,
lifting his chin skyward,
traveling the sun's precocious rays.

June 20, 2001

I slipped again. After a rather rough morning—one
more ripple from my ancient shipwreck—I took a midday
walk deep in the woods.

I walked until I went back in time. Then I walked
some more until I moved out of time. A multitude of
sounds came at me like velvet bats in a great cave. My
hearing magnified. I heard anew.

Listen. God is not silent. God whistles and sings,
hoots and talks in deep, hushed tones in the woods. The
many sounds dance through air, and then weave through
and thread tight the atoms of leaf and bark, soil and grass.
There is a piece. There is a whole living scene. One thing
is everything, everything is fitted together. Nothing is
apart. There is absolutely no room for isolation within the
beating heart of a summer forest.

I walked deeper still. Here all the separate intelligences interlaced effortlessly in a knot of clear being, not unlike grace. The gypsy moth, the thrush, the pond duck, the purple dragonfly, the squirrel, the robin, the dancing white trinity of butterflies in a flutter of love, the raccoon, the human, the carpenter ants, the sycamore, the younger white elm, the frog, the blackbird, I saw them all. They all saw me. We overlapped together in a prayer fold, a prayer fold ushered by the spirit-wind. We were held by something that is ceaseless, and yet still within its many motions.

So I walked inside this green grace, this summer field of benefaction, needing to speak to God after my rough and unpleasant morning. I had come looking.

Wondrously—or perhaps quite naturally—God spoke back. To my great good fortune, I had disappeared, and so was able to hear. And to listen.

June 21, 2001

I am an active supporter of the Nature Conservancy, World Wildlife and other environmental organizations. It is a worthwhile effort, fighting to reclaim and sanctify our beautiful prairies, woodlands, oceans, wetlands—our world.

But it is for our own species that we act. Because in the long run, and sooner than later, Nature will stand triumphant over us pestering homo sapiens. Nature will be muddied, bloodied, despoiled and sooted, but it will not be subdued. Cities, vast cities, countless towns and entire nation states will disappear, yet the earth will spin on, and renew. We will disappear, the earth will remain. New life will sprout.

We will succeed only in evicting ourselves from this most beautiful of homes.

The earth will remain, we may not.

It is a sobering thought, but to me, a refreshing one too.

June 29, 2001

Standing still for just a moment, the house quiet, the summer new, the sun streaming through seemingly every window, everything separate dissolves.

For a glorious moment there are no more plans, no more have-to's, no more bright ideas, no more disappointments, no expectations, no loss, no gain.

It is just light swimming in light.

It is just a gentle spin on the shoulders of the world.

It is just this.

July 5, 2001

Dead is dead. Then again it ain't.

The dead tend to speak to us in a variety of ways. Not only do we still live with the legacy of the dead, we carry them in pockets in our brain. Yes, our ancestors live on in the works they have done, the buildings they have built, and the genes and the stories they have passed on. But more than that, the dead, especially the accomplished dead, are suddenly the wisest beings walking down the block. We tend to screw their heads on in place of our own.

We think that people who lived before us—even long before us—knew the ropes, and that we do not. Most peoples have looked back at civilizations that are no longer extant, seeing them as the last true home of wisdom and grace. Once a culture or a person dies, we actually take them seriously, and listen to what they have to say. Strange, isn't it?

It is wholly worthwhile to hear—and listen to— Dogen's voice, Shakespeare's, Lincoln's, Einstein's,

Maezumi Roshi's. But we need be careful here. Who is it that is actually speaking? From whence does this wisdom spring forth? Where does final authority lie? How profound is our distrust for the blood that flows in our veins, our own living wisdom? And what, exactly, do these brilliant dearly departed have to tell us that the singing cricket I met the other day does not?

July 14, 2001

Water. Acorns. Stones. A nest.
What is it to be a human being?

Our eyes open. We look about. Here are rivers, raspberries, bananas, fish, maple trees, avocados, mud, hay, timber, taro root, oxen, horses, sheep, jungle, palm, rain, macadamia nuts, ocean. How is that homo sapiens sapien creates such difficulty for itself? For countless generations there have been tools, towns, agriculture, fishing, and fire. But once survival is reasonably assured, why is it that we continue to harass and harm other beings, other than the occasional requirement for complex amino acids in the form of warm flesh proteins?

Can we locate that critical border? Precisely where does curiosity, invention, a sense of adventure, ship building, the migration of peoples, establishing a new homeland, the wish to provide a better life for one's children, and the construction of a ten room house somehow become the land of disenchantment and dissatisfaction? What is it about the way we perceive our world that estranges us from it? Our minds create hungers above and beyond our already satisfied needs. We are always getting up and going on the prowl for God-knows-what. We are always grabbing for more.

Why is that?

How closely connected are aggressiveness and adventuring? Are they like the intertwined strands of our very DNA? Does ensuring the survival of our precious offspring sometimes dictate that they live and that others do not? Precisely what kind of beast is able to build a city filled with markets, fountains and fine art, and then blow that city to smithereens? I am so perplexed by this animal that listens to the music of Mozart or the happy banging of tribal drums, and then grabs a machete or a machine gun, and runs out the door to destroy other musicians, teachers, poets, parents, farmers, or fishermen.

So how do the more pacifistic, more enlightened societies survive? Tibet remained largely isolated in its high mountain home for centuries, but was no match for the marauding Chinese just over forty years ago. If Shakers are peaceful people but they do not have offspring, and if noble, well practiced Buddhists are respectful and generous of heart and deed to one another, but can not defend themselves, and so are wiped out . . .

I digress. Then again, perhaps the Shaolin monks trained to defend themselves with the rough and capable "empty hand" of kung fu were not unwise. Of course, there are still many millions of Buddhists in our world, so two and one half millennia of conflict and war did not wipe them out as yet. But I digress once again . . .

What is it to be a human being? I pour a cup of coffee, appreciate the warm black bean going down an open throat, and listen out of one ear to Joni Mitchell singing about lost love, while out of the other ear I hear the Phantom jets of our rich and democratic homeland flying overhead, traveling east, out toward the great ocean, on their way to other lands.

August 11, 2001

Enlightened Eros. It is a wet planet, voluptuous and ripe. It is verdant, fruity and giving. Its mossy green hills are largely kind. Its mix of wind, earth, fire and air are lusty-full, life-affirming, exciting, electric.

It is not just a sex-obsessed society, its a sex drenched life, planet, universe. There is vast longing and endless coupling.

Our lids close, our eyes roll back, and the sky splits open. It is raining love and a wondrous sex, both wild and gentle, from all corners of the galaxy.

September 8, 2001

Somehow a small fly or gnat is squashed and stuck to the lower left on this page of my journal. I study it as I write this; or perhaps we are watching each other, despite the fact that he's dead.

On a beautiful September day with my beautiful son, all of us well, well fed, with more stuff than we can possibly use, I am smack in the middle of dhukka, a sense of lack, of unsatisfactoriness, of something missing, of being less than complete.

Yes, it is our affluent, spoiled, overabundant lifestyle. Yes, it is our grasping, greedy monkey mind, Yes, it is the clash of constant marketing, high expectations, low self esteem, and a culture that daily promotes: This is not it! You want *that*! You want something different! You, my friend, need more!

And of course, you can work to quiet the mind, or you can grasp, gain, grasp, gain, grasp, lose, go for that, and *that*, and remain perpetually dissatisfied, until you wind up like that little fellow to the left, which will be soon enough.

September 15, 2001

Nearly everyone's perspective changed after our great national tragedy.

We were going to ride our stock portfolios into blissful early retirement. We were going to keep jogging and gyming and riding the rapids in Colorado. We were going to fix our teeth and wear soft contacts. We were going to leave our therapy sessions only to do some yoga, insight meditation or tai-chi. We were going to play with our children vigorously and often, and keep our own extended childhoods going into this new millennium and into our fifth or sixth decade. We children of the forties, fifties and early sixties were still truckin', still playin', still partyin', still smokin' self-congratulatory cigars, still sippin' triple distilled vodka, still dancin' past midnight, still rockin'.

But someone just blew up the jukebox.

October 30, 2001

On doing battle.

Yes, the world is created for each of us by our own minds. Yes, the illusion of separateness is just that, and yet when is it simplistic to sit in private quietude and when is it holy to face danger and fight?

There is more at stake here than our own peaceful presence.

Is it holy, as in wholly appropriate and just, to fight for your children, wife, family, friends and neighbors? We admire sacrifice when an adult pushes a child out of the way of an oncoming vehicle only to be stuck himself, do we not?

I am not a vegetarian. Neither am I a pacifist. I admire both, but I am not of their ranks. I see that there are times when one can not simply cover one's eyes and pray. There are times we must protect what is precious. My teacher says the dharma is rare, and precious. Yet if those who practice and live the dharma are wiped out, how helpful is the dharma when it is only in the air and in the soil?

These are also precious: democracy and pluralism, religious freedom and freedom of speech; our fathers and mothers and brothers and sisters are precious. Our children's safety is precious. We will all die, so I proclaim that is indeed worth dying for freedom, science and the 500 year Western Enlightenment, for civil liberties and women's rights, for baseball and Shakespeare in the park, for cinema and space travel, for our homes and home-land—the beautiful breadbasket that feeds a large number of people in this world and that has taken in many millions of the oppressed and persecuted for over 300 years. It is worth dying to preserve our Supreme Court and our national parks, to safeguard San Francisco, New York City, Dallas and Peoria. Human freedom, human dignity and the Constitution are all worth dying for.

That said, we need to be equally bold and careful. We need to be like skilled surgeons. For the death of which Afghani, Arab or Iraqi child, woman or old person will help ensure our safety and freedom? Who are we to eliminate; and once eliminated, whose absence will ensure that we remain a free, just, generous and compassionate peoples?

When the Nazis and terrorists come, our courage is tested. But our wisdom is tested all the more. We need to remember the battle of D-Day and the liberation of Europe, but we also need to remember the Marshall Plan in post-war Europe and the helpful way we taught the defeated Japanese about democracy and commerce from 1946 on.

November 7, 2001

Less than two months later we are beginning to heal. We are a resilient species.

While we are here, the opportunity to be revived and made whole is with us at all times. Also, I love American optimism. It is one of our many national blessings.

My practice? It is perfectly imperfect. I jog and go to the gym, and I am in good shape, but I have never entered a marathon or a body building competition. I am better off, in body and mind, for the running, weight lifting, swimming and yoga. That is enough. Zazen is preferable to no meditation. Even in the realm of cobalt blue high atmosphere skies, where distinctions are transparent, mindful activity is preferable to sloth.

I read Tricycle magazine and Dogen. I sit at home or at the monastery in Mount Tremper—my idealism planted with my side yard tomatoes, now withered vine and dust—and I confront my mind, and occassionally quiet it. Satori might as well be Oz. I appreciate the Buddha in my cerebellum and in my stomach, and I relish his presence in me. I eat. I jog. I go to work and design brochures. I go to the movies. I bicker with my wife. I hug my wife. I go shopping. I sit.

I am neither endlessly striving, nor am I retired. The good air always circulates.

Sometimes I stick my face in the refreshing winds that blow my way, other days I fan myself. I look up at the cosmos, I look in at it. There's really not much I need do.

November 19, 2001

That which comes
at us
is us.
Winter.
Spring.
Summer.
Fall.

The door
is always
open.

December 21, 2001, Santa Fe, New Mexico

It is one thing to appreciate one's life, it is another to demonstrate and extend that appreciation.

It is one thing to have great realization, it is another to actualize that realization, and share it, and take down the fence between me and you, mine and yours.

Then again, it *is* one thing, it is always one thing, and the one thing is whole and unlimited and vibrant and full of more change than all nickels, dimes and quarters in the metal dispenser on the hip of the happy ice cream man.

December 22, 2001

My young son and I entered Saint Francis church in Santa Fe on a whim as I was strolling him through town. It was early Saturday morning, and so we watched many of the practitioners decorate the beautiful interior of the church with poinsettia and a large tree for the coming Christmas service. We sat in a pew by ourselves and watched the happy busyness, and took in the grand spaces of this exquisite southwestern chapel. It was then that I noticed a plaque which read:

Love One Another Constantly.

It stopped me cold. *Constantly*? How do we love one another constantly?

You know. Your heart knows. For our hearts beat wisely, and have never quite bought into the illusion of separateness.

When I am seated in my heart and I am more than me, then I can love you constantly.

December 30, 2001

Knee and heart are humming,
As the world just fell off the ledge.
And all the crows are singing,
There is no edge. There is no edge.

Glossary

Big Mind: Similar to Buddha nature; the ultimate, the unified Absolute as opposed to the relative particulars; an allegory for the absolute intimacy between all of life and the interrelatedness of all sentient beings.

boddhicitta: The awakened heart, or the mind that aspires to realization; it is the innate impulse that motivates people to strive for a deeper understanding of the nature of reality.

Bodhisattva: "Enlightenment Being" or "Pure-minded One"; an awakened being who chooses to delay entry into Nirvana until everyone, all beings, are liberated. In everyday terms, one who uses their compassionate realization to eliminate suffering in the world, and to assist others in their awakening.

Buddha nature: A phrase that points to our true nature; that which is complete and unadorned, the underlying Being or essence within; or the inherently awakened state which resides within earthly forms and all of nature.

chi: breath, energy, lifeforce.

daisan/dokusan: a private, one-on-one interview between student and teacher to explore the student's understanding of the dharma.

Dharma: since there is no direct English translation of this Sanskrit word, it has often been translated as (Buddhist) religious law, but it is more akin to Natural Law, as in a living imperative or a fundamental quality. Generally, it is used as the word to connote the sum of the Buddha's teachings.

dhukka: The perpertual state of dissatisfaction; the suffering and dread that arises from our desires and fears; existential apprehension or anguish.

Dogen, Eihei: Zen master who lived in Japan from 1200-1253, founder of the Soto sect of Zen (the other remaining sect is Rinzai, which is more inclined to use koan study and to emphasize striving for sudden realization). Soto, which also uses some koan study, is more likely to promote a seemingly contradictory philosophy of perfect, already existent enlightenment and a student's gradual awakening to this truth. A highly regarded philosopher of metaphysics and ontology, a Zen teacher, and founder of a still flourishing monastery, Dogen is also known for his prolific writings, especially Shobogenzo.

The Four Noble Truths: The primary teaching of the Buddha; that life is largely suffering; second, there is a cause for this suffering, which is ego, greed and thus perpetual dissatisfaction; third, there is a way to understand and transform this suffering; and finally, that the roadmap to end suffering is the Buddha's detailed Eightfold Path of Right Concentration, Right Mindfulness, Right Intention, Right Speech, Right Action, Right Practice, Right Views, and Right Livelihood ("Right" meaning appropriate, aware and caring, as opposed to the one and only right way to do something).

Gassho: Bringing the palms of the hands together, usually with a slight bow, as a sign of respect and intimacy; the word is sometimes used as a salutation at the end of a correspondence.

Gateless Gate: A phrase that is used as an allegory for entry into a deeper study of the self; the ever present opening to *The Way*; and a classic Zen text by Mu-mon. His *No-gate-barrier* was written in China in the 1200s, and contained a series of small anecdotes and allegorical tales, usually concerning discussions between teachers and students.

The Great Matter: The phrase used to acknowledge our mortality; it also points to the examination and eventual piercing of the twin mysteries of birth and death; including how they are related, and how they too are not quite what they seem.

Home Leaving: Refers to one literally leaving home and family behind to seek a deeper understanding and eventual enlightenment, which Siddhartha Gautauma, the Buddha, actually did; leaving his wife, child, royal family and clan behind to embark upon his spiritual quest. It is also a metaphor for leaving one's past and the things of the world behind during a retreat or a spiritual journey.

Hotei: The happy Buddha of Japan; this forever smiling, rotund figure, usually portrayed shirtless and with his big bag of sweets and toys for children, is an embodiment of the wise Fool, an egoless being filled with great generosity, a soul without a care in the world.

karma: Means "doing," and refers to the world of cause and effect; the consequence of one's actions. It also refers to our wilfullness and intention, and how our actions affect everything from our immediate behavior to those around us and the rest of the world.

kensho: An insight experience; a brief but meaningful glimpse into one's true nature; a tantalizing taste of realization.

kinhin: walking meditation; it usually follows zazen or seated meditation, acting as a transition from stillness to activity.

koan: a statement or question, and often a brief Zen tale, which is posed in the spirit of a riddle, for the purpose of confronting and knocking off balance our everyday dualistic thinking in order to promote a more intuitive and holistic understanding, so one may grasp the matter at hand by one's very life and not just by one's intellect.

kyosaku stick: a long, flat stick which both reinvigorates the tired meditator and stimulates the trapezoidal muscles which it hits (a brief, self-directed, slightly startling, but helpful ouch).

Mahayana: One of the three mains branches of the Buddhist religion (the other being Hinayana or Theravadan, the third, Vajrayana); it translates as the "Greater Vehicle" and its primary tenets include the infinite quality of Buddha nature and the dharma throughout all of space and time; the interconnectedness between all of existence and all beings; and the special responsibility or inclination an enlightened being has to remain involved with the world; to guide others and transmit True Nature and the dharma to other beings who are not yet realized.

Mu: Often the first koan a student receives: "Does a dog have Buddha nature? Answer: "Mu!" Mu can equally mean "without" or be an ambiguous response, not unlike, "Well, not quite, but perhaps."

Nirvana (Sanskrit): "Extinguishing," as in blowing out a candle; in Theravadan Buddhism it usually implies union with the Absolute and the cessation of suffering; while in Mahayana, and Zen particularly, it is more subtle and refers to the inherent emptiness of form; that the objects and life forms of this existence, the relative, contain the Absolute; and further, like "eternity in a dewdrop," that the Absolute is not separate from the relative sphere. It also refers to the diminishment of day-to-day karma and its effects through non-attachment and egolessness.

Original Face: From the koan, "What was your Original Face before you were born?" Original Face refers to True Nature or Buddha nature; to origin and essence.

the ox: Often refers to self-discipline, the effort of focusing one's energies toward self realization. In Zen there are ten famous Ox-herding pictures, drawings which depict the "10 stages" of enlightenment; from the search for the ox, taming the ox, up to eventual transcendence of seeker and that which is sought.

Prajna Paramita: Virtuous knowledge or unsurpassable wisdom; striving for a state of being which is already present (Sanskrit: "reaching the other shore"); or, wisdom which is fully experienced in the present and not merely glimpsed or conceived.

samadhi: a focused state of concentration, the single-pointedness of zazen, which can lead to an open, conception-free, judgment-free state of being; often referred to as "dropping away of body and mind."

satori: complete awakening; the experience of true selflessness, or of a fully transparent self; a sudden, irrevocable experience of Big Mind and unblemished clear mindedness; a being in full, having sheer intimacy with all of existence and the ever transforming lifeforce.

sensei: Japanese for teacher or an adept; a master

sesshin: Japanese for "gathering the heart-mind"; it is an intensive meditation retreat, usually three to seven days, which involves silence, restrictions on social interaction, ceremonial meals known as Oryoki ("just enough"), and long hours of meditation.

shikantaza: Japanese for "only sitting;" which refers to sitting in meditation in a relaxed, receptive state; simple sitting as opposed to counting the breath or wrestling with a koan during meditation.

Siddhartha Gautauma: The historical Buddha, was born in northern India in what is now Nepal about 560 years before the birth of Jesus; also known as Shakyamuni, the sage of the Shakya clan, of which his father was leader, and he a prince. Sometime in his late 20s he left home and tribe to spend six or seven years engaged in various, often extreme ascetic practices for the purpose of understanding the causes of suffering and the mysteries of birth, existence and death. After achieving his complete awakening (Buddha means awakened one), he traveled the countryside, espousing a philosophy of "the Middle Way" which suggested avoiding the two extremes of a life devoted solely to harsh restrictions and self denial, and equally, avoiding a life devoted only to pleasure, acquisition and self satisfaction. He taught on the nature of the self, non-attachment or not clinging, compassion for all fellow beings, and ways to reduce human suffering for nearly 50 years. Never claiming any sort of divine status, but rather the opposite, and exhorting his followers to test his teachings empirically, by and for themselves, in their own lives, and to remain always "a lamp unto one's self," he taught numerous gatherings and individuals until passing away at age 80.

tathata (Sanskrit): suchness, thusness; just this, the state of things in the moment; Tathagatha ("the one thus gone") is another name for the Buddha.

sunyata (or shunyata): No-thing; the Void; the open space of pure possibility.

the Tao: Chinese for The Way; the universal principle; the nature of things; the flow of existence and the cycles of life.

the Ten Thousand Things: all the phenomena of existence; the many beings, plants, elements and objects of this world; the world of appearances.

Theravadan (and Vajrayana): The Doctrine of the Elders, is the oldest branch of Buddhism; which arose from those monks and followers who succeeded the historical Buddha, and which stresses the study of the Buddha's spoken teachings and ancient Buddhist canons; the importance of monastic tradition and ethical conduct; and the cultivation of individuals into fully realized beings, originally known in India as an arhat, a being of great merit. The third major school of Buddhism, Vajrayana, colorfully known as "the way of the firm and unyielding bolt of thunder," is a branch of Mahayana. Vajrayana is the expression which took root in Tibet, mixing there centuries ago with preexisting nature, spirit, oracle and trance cults to create the rich and multi-layered Tibetan Buddhism we see today.

the Void: The principal of no-thing-ness, that matter is ultimately without absolute substance, that it is but a form of ceaseless change and energy, and that energy itself is without real substance. This is the great Nothing, an allegory for a non-dual state of existence, from which all things — the formed and the formless, the singular and the composite — spring and to which all things return, only to endlessly transform.

zazen: Seated meditation; focused, silent awareness.

zazenkai: A one-day meditation retreat.

zendo: A large hall or any designated room for meditation.

KEN TAUB is an advertis-
ing executive, creative di-
rector, and copywriter.
Before his career in ad-
vertising, he received his
B.A. in Chinese Studies at
the University of San Di-
ego, with post-graduate
studies at the Monterey
Institute of International
Studies. He lives with his
wife and son in St. James, New York.

Wisdom Literature from White Cloud Press

The Buddha: The Story of An Awakened Life
by David Kherdian
ISBN: 1-883991-63-3 / Paperback: $14.95

America Needs a Buddhist President
Text by Brett Bevell, Illustrations by Eben Dodd
ISBN: 1-883991-97-8 / Paperback: $8.95

The Buddha Smiles: A Collection of Dharmatoons
by Mari Gayatri Stein
ISBN: 1-883991-28-5 / Paperback: $15.95

Wild Grace: Nature as a Spiritual Path
by Eric Alan
ISBN: 1-883991-53-6 / Paperback: $16.95

Creating Consciousness: A Study of Consciousness, Creativity, Evolution, and Violence
by Albert Low
ISBN: 1-883991-39-0 / Paperback: $18.95

Yin Yoga: Outline of a Quiet Practice
by Paul Grilley
ISBN: 1-883991-43-9 / Paperback: $15.95

Ways in Mystery: Explorations of Mystical Awareness and Life
by Luther Askeland
ISBN: 1-883991-16-1 / Paperback: $17.00

For more information on these and other titles, visit:
www.whitecloudpress.com

White Cloud Press
Ashland, Oregon